BETWEENWORLDS

VOYAGERS TO BRITAIN 1700–1850

BETWEEN
WORLDS
VOYAGERS TO BRITAIN 1700–1850

Jocelyn Hackforth-Jones

David Bindman
Romita Ray
Stephanie Pratt

Foreword by
Ekow Eshun

National Portrait Gallery, London

Published in Great Britain by National Portrait Gallery
Publications, National Portrait Gallery, St Martin's Place,
London WC2H 0HE

Published to accompany the exhibition *Between Worlds:
Voyagers to Britain 1700–1850* held at the National Portrait
Gallery, London, from 8 March to 17 June 2007.

For a complete catalogue of current publications please
write to the address above, or visit our website at
www.npg.org.uk/publications

Publishing Manager: Celia Joicey
Project Editor: Johanna Stephenson
Senior Editor: Anjali Bulley
Picture Research: Dominique Monteil
Production Manager: Ruth Müller-Wirth
Design: Rose-Innes Associates

ISBN 13: 978 1 85514 379 1
ISBN 10: 1 85514 379 8

A catalogue record for this book is available from the
British Library.

The publisher would like to thank the copyright holders
for granting permission to reproduce works illustrated
in this book. Every effort has been made to contact the
holders of copyright material, and any omissions will
be corrected in future editions if the publisher is notified
in writing.

Frontispiece
Maharaja Dalip Singh (detail)
Franz Xaver Winterhalter, 1854
The Royal Collection

Contents

Director's Foreword

There is nothing mysterious or natural about authority. It is formed, irradiated, disseminated; it is instrumental, it is persuasive; it has status, it establishes canons of taste and value; it is virtually indistinguishable from certain ideas it dignifies as true, and from traditions, perceptions and judgements it forms, transmits, reproduces. Above all, authority can, and indeed must, be analyzed.
Edward Said, *Orientalism*, New York, 1978, p. 19

However beautiful or telling the result, the circumstance of a portrait is sometimes authoritarian and at worst exploitative. A portrait can be understood as a moment of definition as well as tracing an element of performance, when the subject poses under instruction from an artist within the conventions of a foreign land. And like a theatrical performance, a portrait may offer different levels of interaction for the viewer and the person viewed. Masquerade plays a part in all portraiture and performance, and some elements are constructed for the portraits in this exhibition. What cannot be seen in the portrait may be just as important as what is immediately visible.

Between Worlds focuses on a number of moments of portraiture – each constrained by some form of authority – which relate to stories that are both bold and shocking. The circumstance for each of these subjects in travelling to London was rarely benign. The background of colonial development, exploitation and warfare is well known, but what is often less clear or simply lost in a larger narrative is the personal situation of the subjects, including their determination, as emissaries or as representatives, to maintain human dignity beyond the everyday matters of how they were addressed or remarked upon.

Great myths, from the Norse voyages to the Greek epics, include the discovery of other people, and a fascination with those from other societies is common to most people. Yet the exotic remains a realm of intrigue as well as being tinged with the discomfort of racist attitudes or stereotypes. To understand fully the images of others may be impossible, but with the attempt comes understanding and mutual respect.

I should like to thank all those who have worked hard to realise this project, most particularly Jos Hackforth-Jones who initiated and developed the idea. I am also grateful to the curatorial team working with her – David Bindman, Romita Ray and Stephanie Pratt – who have created a wonderful exhibition and publication. I should also like to thank Peter Funnell and Claire Everitt, colleagues at the National Portrait Gallery, who have both made special contributions to the project, and Joanna Banham, Pim Baxter, Anjali Bulley, Andrea Easey, Denise Ellitson, Neil Evans, Celia Joicey, Ian Gardner, Dominique Monteil, Ruth Müller-Wirth, Grita Rose-Innes, Jonathan Rowbotham, David Saywell, Johanna Stephenson, Sarah Tinsley, Rosie Wilson and many others in the Communication and Development, Learning and Access, and Exhibitions departments who have contributed to its realisation.

Sandy Nairne *Director*
National Portrait Gallery, London

Foreword

Before satellites, before aeroplanes, before telephone lines, travellers ploughed between the continents on tall-masted ships, subject to the vagaries of waves and ocean currents. Let's imagine for a moment that in the centuries of those journeys, Columbus hailing sight of America in 1492, a Portuguese ship commanded by captain Diego d'Azambuja erecting the first European settlement on African soil a decade earlier, the wake lines of those ships were captured on the surface of the sea. What would we witness but a lattice of connections scored into the waves linking the people and continents of the world? From such a web, the start or destination point of a journey would be much less apparent than the fact of the connection between two distant lands. And viewed in this way, the story of those connections becomes far less that of Enlightened Europe encountering the New World and the Dark Continent, and much more a chronicle of mutual discoveries in which individuals and cultures and eventually whole continents are changed by the repercussions of connection.

Between Worlds is about eighteenth- and nineteenth-century encounters. But it is also very much about Britain today. How else could it be when in London alone there are some 300 different languages spoken every day? And when, with varying shades of earnestness and angst, the shifting demography of Britain is pored over each day in lavish detail, its racial and ethnic particularities, its immigration problems and cultural paradoxes. The stories that unfold every day are indicative of a nation intermittently at ease and at odds with its shifting make-up. Newspaper business pages laud a British-born teenager of Nigerian parentage who has become a mobile phone ringtone millionaire; tabloid headlines decry an alleged invasion of Eastern European Roma; TV reports ponder how four British-Asian young men could turn into the country's first suicide bombers.

And it was ever thus. Racial and ethnic difference is marked in this country with generous degrees of boosterism and suspicion. *Between Worlds* details some of those stories; but even as far back as 1601, Queen Elizabeth I was wondering aloud, with some acidity, whether the 'great number of negars and Blackamoors' in Britain did not threaten to destroy the sanctity of her realm.

Here's a question. Where are you from? No, where are you really from? I ask because it has been posed to me through most of my life and I am still to find a wholly satisfactory answer. I could say, I am Ghanaian. That I am British but my parents are from Ghana. That I am a Londoner, born and bred. Or indeed that they are true en masse and that any single one of them is only partially so.

The question matters because it is the one bequeathed to us by the encounters described in *Between Worlds* and the other centuries of connection across the latticed surface of the world. As my response goes some way to show, the answer to it is no simple matter. Many of us who were born and live in Britain have a similarly complicated reply to a straightforward query. Racially or culturally, many – indeed, I'd say most – of us can trace our origins to more than one place. Britain is a hybrid nation, an island that has come into being out of comings and goings across the ocean. Walk down any street in any city in this country and you will see the results of those journeys. You will see a nation that is not simply one colour, one belief. You will see a nation united by difference. For all that politicians or commentators descry that mixing, for all that there have been resentments and riots and yes, now even suicide bombings – for all that, Britain is home to the cultures of many rather than the property of a native few. In the end, my answer to the question of where are you really from comes down to a single word: here. Which is to say that, as the child of immigrants, I recognise the mutability of nationality and the act of choice that goes into making a country your own. I am from here, Britain. And in choosing to bind myself to this place, I also bring it that little bit closer to me, in character, culture and colour. The same is true of all the other children and descendants of immigrants within its boundaries. They have made an active choice to live here, giving of some of their customs and culture to its whole. In doing so, the nation shifts. It makes itself over time and again, with each beat of the current against its shores.

Many of the stories chronicled in *Between Worlds* are brief encounters, tales of travellers whose journeys ultimately returned them to their own homes. What no one at the time could have imagined was the consequence of those journeys: the fact that, in their wake, the Britain they left behind would never be the same again.

Ekow Eshun *Artistic Director*
Institute of Contemporary Arts, London

Fig. 1 **Omai (Mai)**
Sir Joshua Reynolds, 1775–6
Oil on canvas
2360 x 1455 mm (92⅞ x 57¼")
Private collection

Introduction

Jocelyn Hackforth-Jones

Indigenous perceptions of, and reactions to, foreign people and their goods must be taken seriously.[1]

From the seventeeth century, largely as a result of British colonial expansion, a number of non-European individuals from distant lands visited, or were brought to, London and were objects of excitement, interest and curiosity. This book and the accompanying exhibition consider the complexities and ambiguities of their encounters during their sojourn, and focus on the relationships that were forged across cultural boundaries. For the most part they were people of some status, either in their own cultures or in their negotiations 'between cultures' while in London. The following chapters consider nine narratives of men and women drawn to London from regions with which Britain had a colonial relationship: namely North America, the South Pacific, Africa and India.

These narratives also bear witness to the cultural diversity of London for at least the last three hundred years and make a space for an investigation of the subtleties in relationships and attitudes across cultures. While many view London's multicultural history as a phenomenon that began in the 1950s, in fact the city has had a diverse cultural population for several hundred years. Over two hundred years ago in *The Prelude* (1805) the poet William Wordsworth recalled his excitement on returning to London after three years in Cambridge:

> Now homeward through the thickening hubbub …
> The Hunter-Indian; Moors,
> Malays, Lascars, the Tartar, the Chinese
> And Negro Ladies in white muslin Gowns.

The visibility of the black inhabitants of London in Wordsworth's day was far in excess of their small numbers. Their image was pervasive, both in the more popular reproduced imagery such as prints by artists including Hogarth, Gillray and Rowlandson, and on tavern, coffee-house and shop signs.[2] As a metropolis with a diverse cultural and ethnic population dating back several hundred years, London was ideally suited to the narratives of encounter examined here.

For the art historians engaged in this project the points of access have generally been European records: paintings, prints, watercolours, books, poems, letters and pamphlets. Where objects from the material culture of the visitors are analysed, it is generally as 'artificial curiosities' (the eighteenth-century term for ethnographic artefacts),[3] and to illuminate both European visual imagery and the complexity of encounters. A case in point is the discussion in Chapter 1 of the powerful political and sacred symbolism of the wampum belt held by one of the 'Four Indian Kings'. For the most part, however, the perspective of the writers here is European.

What is striking for the contemporary viewer is the consistency of elite modes of representation of these visitors. With the exception of Bennelong and Sara Baartman, all are represented by oil paintings, in many cases painted by the leading portrait artists of the day including Sir Godfrey Kneller, John Verelst, Sir Joshua Reynolds, George Romney and Franz Xaver Winterhalter. The 'surprise of recognition' for the viewer frequently lies in the use of conventional European modes of portrayal to represent non-Europeans. Thus Kneller's large-scale portrait of Michael Alphonsus Shen Fu-Tsung (1687; fig. 2), a Chinese convert to Christianity, emphasises the sitter's conversion – he is portrayed in Chinese robes, holding up a crucifix and gazing into the distance.[4]

A number of circumstances connected with British colonial exploration and subsequent imperial expansion drew these travellers to London. Members of various North American communities travelled to the city as early as the sixteenth century. One of the first and most celebrated to initiate the practice of dignitaries being brought to London was Pocahontas (fig. 3), the daughter of a leading figure of her tribe; brought to England by her English husband, she made quite an impression when she was presented at court.

In 1710 the so-called Four Indian Kings travelled to London as diplomatic and

According to Horace Walpole, of all his works this was the one of which Kneller was the most proud. Shen Fu-Tsung was the child of prosperous Chinese Christian parents and as a result of the intervention of Father Philip Couplet, Procurator of the China Jesuits in Rome, he travelled to Europe in 1681. In England he became well known in court circles and helped to catalogue the Chinese manuscripts in the Bodleian Library.

Fig. 2 **Michael Alphonsus Shen Fu-Tsung, 'The Chinese Convert'**
Sir Godfrey Kneller, 1687
Oil on canvas
2121 x 1320 mm (83 ½ x 52")
The Royal Collection

Fig. 3 **Pocahontas**
After Simon de Passe
Published 1793
Line engraving
172 x 146 mm (6¾ x 5¾")
National Portrait Gallery,
London

cultural emissaries representing their people, with a view to forging a closer alliance with the British who were fighting the French for control of the North American continent. Over sixty years later, in 1775, Joseph Brant or Thayendanegea (his Mohawk name) made his first visit to London, to draw up a treaty with the British on behalf of his people. In 1785, shortly after the Treaty of Paris had been signed between the recently formed United States Government and the British, Brant returned again to London to represent Mohawk interests and to remind the English of their duty to their American Indian allies. Brant's second visit may also be seen in the context of the influx of black visitors from North America to London at this time. While it is estimated that there were never more than about 10,000 black people at any time in eighteenth-century England, during the 1780s this number rose to accommodate the large numbers of black Americans who had been promised their freedom in return for supporting the British cause in North America.[5]

If these American Indian visits reinforced the imperative for the British to engage and negotiate with representatives of native peoples in the course of the eighteenth century, the circumstances surrounding the arrival in 1748 of the African Sessarakoo remind us of the violence and human exploitation behind both internal and external colonial expansion. Sessarakoo had been sent on a European Grand Tour by his father, a wealthy West African slave-trader, but had himself been

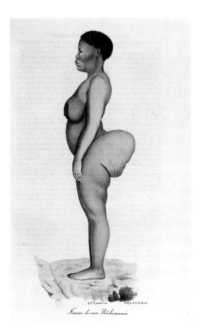

Fig. 4 'The Hottentot Venus, Bushman Woman'
Carel Christian Last, 1824
From *L'Histoire Naturelle des Mammifères* by Etienne Geoffroy Saint-Hilaire and Frédéric Cuvier
Colour lithograph
483 x 335 mm (19 x 13⅛")
Bibliothèque Nationale, Paris

captured and sold into slavery in Barbados. By the time he arrived in London he was already a celebrity, familiar (one assumes) with many aspects of the trade in slaves. His high rank and the sympathy and hospitality shown to him by London society differentiated him from the majority of his compatriots who were slaves in domestic service. The Tahitian (or more properly Raiatean, since he came from the neighbouring island of Raiatea) Mai was brought to London in 1774 as a result of British colonial voyages of exploration and expansion then prevalent – in this instance Captain James Cook's second voyage of exploration. He, too, was presented at court and became a celebrated figure in London drawing rooms, occupying a position somewhere between ethnographic specimen, gentleman and cultural emissary with (as we shall see) his own set of agendas.

Approximately twenty years later, in 1793, the Aborigines Bennelong and Yemmerrawanne were brought to London by Captain Arthur Phillip, the first Governor of the penal colony recently established in New South Wales. While both men accompanied Phillip voluntarily and were also presented at court, they appear not to have made the impression that the earlier visitors had. This may reflect both a shift in attitudes to native peoples, who were increasingly regarded merely as ethnographic specimens from outposts of the Empire, and a gradual decline in the popular image of the Noble Savage.

Fig. 5 **Rammohun Roy**
Rembrandt Peale, 1833
Oil on canvas
985 x 855 mm (38¾ x 33⅝″)
Peabody Essex Museum

The circumstances of Sara Baartman's removal to England suggest that she, too, was of interest primarily as a 'curious' ethnographic specimen (fig. 4). Baartman was a member of the Khoikhoi, South Africa's first indigenous people. She was exhibited in a public show in Piccadilly, London, between 1810 and 1814. Such acts, and the consequent depiction of Baartman in prints and caricatures, are a powerful reminder of their distance from modern sensitivities. The displaying of Baartman in this manner also outraged many of her European contemporaries, however. The African Association brought a court case with the aim of demonstrating that she had been exhibited 'against her consent'. Baartman spoke for herself in court, confirming that she had given her agreement to being put on display; whether this was under duress is less clear. While the circumstances regarding the treatment and reception of Baartman and Bennelong continue to cause pain and distress to many, such evidence as we have indicates that neither saw themselves as victims. As the following chapters reveal, there were also clear instances of resistance to such stereotyping.

The London sojourns of all three of the Indians included here were also inflected by Britain's colonial project. Dean Mahomed had had a career as an officer in the Indian Army. When his commanding officer Godfrey Evan Baker was recalled, Mahomed followed him to Cork in 1784; by the time he arrived in London in 1807

Fig. 6 **Rammohun Roy**
Henry Perronet Briggs, 1832
Oil on canvas
930 x 570 mm (36⅝ x 22½")
Bristol City Museum and
Art Gallery, UK

he had established a reputation as an educated man of letters. The noble social reformer Raja Rammohun Roy (figs 5, 6) travelled to London in 1830 as an emissary to negotiate an increase in the Mughal emperor's pension and to appeal to the Privy Council against the reintroduction of *sati* (see p. 100). But perhaps the most fascinating and complex tale of the relationship between high-born subject and empire is that of Dalip Singh. The last Sikh ruler of the Punjab, he was forced to give up his kingdom and lands at an early age, and subsequently removed from his own culture to Mussoori, where he received a British colonial education. In a sense Singh was himself a metaphor for the colonial project – his title, lands, Sikh religion and language were completely colonised by the British. The shimmering Winterhalter portrait of 1854 (p. 111), painted at the behest of Queen Victoria, creates a chimera of this Indian prince: a ruler in name only, whose cultural identity has been eroded. A further irony in this mode of portrayal of Dalip Singh as a Sikh prince rests in the fact that he no longer bore the traditional emblems of a Sikh.

Many of these exotic visitors were regarded as 'Princes' or 'Kings' by the British, perhaps because they could not always understand or imagine the position they occupied in their native lands (the 'Four Indian Kings' were all referred to as 'King' or 'Emperor'), or it may have been from a desire to romanticise their backgrounds. Similarly, while for many eighteenth-century Londoners the African Sessarakoo may in reality have been the son of a West African slave-trader, his story appeared to echo that of the fictional prince in the popular contemporary novel and play *Oroonoko*.

In some instances the visitor wished to represent himself as coming from a more exalted stratum of society than that he occupied in his own culture: Mai came from the middle class, not the exalted *ari'i* or priestly class he claimed as his own. Clearly some of the visitors also engaged in a strategy to manipulate their identity – often by managing their own visual representation. In the portraits by Parry and Reynolds (pp. 49, 52; fig. 1) Mai has himself dressed in what has been identified as white tapa cloth, a sign of exalted rank. While Rammohun Roy was given the title of Raja by the Mughal Emperor Akbar II and Dalip Singh had inherited princely titles, this was in name only and it is interesting to note that after his meeting in 1854 with Queen Victoria (who was greatly taken with the handsome Indian), Singh was 'promoted' to the rank of European prince.

In their enacting of a number of European rituals we see these individuals not just operating 'between worlds', but frequently engaging in a process of appropriation of British manners and modes of comportment. The degree to which this was a deliberate strategy is explored here. During the eighteenth century the ceremonies, etiquette, customs and manners of London 'society' must have appeared just as exotic to many of the visitors from North America, Africa, the South Pacific and India as the foreigners in turn appeared to their British counterparts. In 1711 the *Spectator* published an account of some letters purportedly left in the lodgings of one of the Four Indian Kings, in which he observed the strange behaviour of the English who are 'carried up and down the streets in little covered Rooms … Their Dress is likewise very barbarous.'

One consistent educated reaction to nearly all of these visitors commends the manner in which they comported themselves as gentlemen. There are many pictures of this 'performance of gentility' whether verbal, literary or visual. Written accounts and visual representations frequently showed the visitors being presented at court. Sessarakoo's high rank meant that he was apparently welcomed in society drawing rooms, and in the portrait by Gabriel Mathias (p. 36) he is shown appropriately attired to be presented to the King. Mai, too, dressed as a European gentleman and appeared able to emulate gentlemanly behaviour in a manner which Fanny Burney (for one) held to be superior to that of many Englishmen. Joseph Brant's gentlemanly behaviour captivated those he encountered, including James Boswell, who commended his 'gentle and quiet' manners. Like Mai, he was also described as wearing only European garments while in England, although the various portraits depict him wearing a hybridised dress derived from both cultures (a regular occurrence in the representation of these visitors). Again like Mai, he appears to have had an agenda for performing in this way: to dispel the perception of American Indians as 'uncouth and unreasonable'. Bennelong was portrayed in gentlemanly attire, but the fragility of the tiny miniature illustrated here (p. 75) is a metaphor for his complex and at times volatile relationship with the British.

Dean Mahomed's travel memoirs (1793) established him as a well-bred man but many of the visual images of him, including that by Thomas Baynes (p. 78), depict him in elegant hybridised dress as an Anglo-Indian gentleman. He also had himself portrayed in Indian court robes; the gloves and the waistcoat indicating his acquisition of English codes of gentility enliven his traditional court dress. Like other visitors, he may also have been making a claim to descent from a more exalted position than that he actually occupied in India (although in his travel memoirs he apparently traced his family back to the Nawabs of Murshidabad), and have been enacting a double mimicry – not only engaged in the performance of gentility, but also claiming to descend from a higher rank.

In the nineteenth century the manners and presentation of such high-born visitors as Raja Rammohun Roy and Dalip Singh delighted London 'society' and court circles respectively. There are a number of accounts of these travellers seeking parallels in Britain for their own secular and sacred practices. In October 1774, when Mai was taken to Cambridge to visit the Senate House and watch the procession of professors, he was reminded of high priests at the ritual centre of Taputapuatea. It is noteworthy that those individuals who came from highly stratified societies such as Mai, Mahomed, Roy and Singh, intuitively understood and could manipulate English society rituals. Bennelong was particularly conscious of his dress as a marker of social occasion. Visual representations and his tailor's bill indicate that he and Yemmerrawanne dressed as gentlemen. However, they both came from an acephalous society, that is, a society without a hierarchical structure, and were thus less inclined to engage in the performances of sociability that were such a feature of Mai's and of the various Indian visitors.

As well as engaging in their own performances, many of the visitors attended theatrical performances (although Mai had to be reassured that theatres were frequented by the very highest strata of society before he would agree to return). The Four Indian Kings were such celebrities that when they visited a public performance of *Macbeth* the play was interrupted so that the Indian men could be re-seated on stage in full view of the audience. Sessarakoo's distress on witnessing a performance of *Oroonoko* affected the audience more powerfully than the play. Thus the spectator also became part of the spectacle, in a process which more broadly reflects the fluidity of encounters and eliding of boundaries that characterised many of the meetings 'between worlds'.

A recurring theme of this book is the manner in which the representation of these visitors was commodified via consumer products such as engravings, books and theatrical productions. The reproduction of many of the portraits enhanced their visibility in the capital and, in common with the ballads, broadsheets, pantomimes and plays inspired by their visits, also helped to sustain interest in them for many years after their departure. Queen Anne commissioned full-length portraits of each of the Four Indian Kings (by John Verelst; pp. 28–9) to record an important diplomatic meeting. All are shown in hybrid costume which references both their European sojourn (the white shirts and red cloaks with gold braiding given to them for their audience with the Queen) and their American Indian identity (their sashes and the wampum belt depicted in the portrait of the so-called Emperor Theyanoguin). While these portraits hung in Kensington Palace during Queen Anne's lifetime, the mezzotint engravings made after the originals were more broadly disseminated. However, they also appeared as curiosities in much cheaper prints such as 'The true Effigies of the Four Indian Kings' (p. 26). In this cruder version each of the figures is represented in more stereotyped terms as the 'savage other'. The sense of hybridity, of the blurring of boundaries between the European and the American Indian that characterised the oil paintings and the mezzotints authorised by the artist, is undermined here by a number of factors: their faces are darkened and all are wearing generic American Indian dress with prominent tattoos and Indian ornamentation, including feathered earrings. In this and a number of other instances the cruder forms of reproduction could reflect a more one-dimensional stereotype of the non-European visitor. The Four Indian Kings also became the subject of a popular ballad that remained current for over a hundred years.

As the following chapters reveal, for some visitors the encounter with the British had negative consequences and resulted in a painful re-entry into their own culture. However, this book and the accompanying exhibition focus on the dynamics of cross-cultural encounters 'between worlds' and seek to illuminate their richness, ambiguity, complexity and contradictions. In a number of instances cultural 'entanglement' during this period meant that both sides could regard the other as exotic and foreign. As we shall see, part of this process of cultural entanglement meant that each side also manipulated and appropriated elements from the other's culture – a practice that continues to this day.[6]

NOTES

1 Thomas 1991, p. 184.

2 See Sandhu 2004 (2003), p. 14 and chapter 1.

3 See Kaeppler 1978.

4 G.A. Bailey, 'Religious Encounter: Christianity in Asia', in *Encounters* 2004.

5 Sandhu 2004 (2003), p. 12.

6 Thomas 1991, p. 184.

1 The Four 'Indian Kings'

Stephanie Pratt

In 1710, during the reign of Queen Anne, four American Indians from what is now eastern New York State left their homeland to visit the English court and forge an alliance. Three of them were Mohawk (in their own language Canienga or 'People of the Flint'), the fourth was Mahican (meaning 'Wolf'). All were members of a greater confederation and alliance of tribal peoples called the Iroquois or, in their own language, Haudenosaunee. Their arrival created a sensation. The 'Four Indian Kings', as they became known, were the talk of London: they sat for their portraits, they were given two audiences with the Queen, they were received by members of the aristocracy and they provoked much speculation on their history, culture and society.[1] They visited public entertainments and on one occasion a performance of *Macbeth* at the Queen's Theatre, Haymarket, had to be interrupted so that the Indian men seated in the front box could be re-seated on stage, in full view of the public.[2]

The Indian Kings fascinated their hosts not merely because American Indian peoples were intrinsically interesting, but also because of their potential to offer lessons about English customs and manners. Indian culture and social practices, insofar

History and Progress of the Four Indian Kings
Published by A. Hinde, 1710
Printed book
Page 195 x 125 mm (7⅝ x 4⅞")
The British Library

Tee Yee Neen Ho Ga Row, Emperor of the Six Nations
John Verelst, 1710
Library and Archives, Canada, acc. no. 1977-35-4. Acquired with a special grant from the Canadian Government, 1977

as they presented alternatives to English behaviour, could be drawn on to make sharp observations about the foibles of life in London in the early eighteenth century. In the *Spectator*, no. 50, of 27 April 1711, Joseph Addison used the Indian Kings' visit as a lens to focus his readers' attention on how the English lived. His account purports to provide extracts from some letters supposedly left in the lodgings of 'King *Sa Ga Yean Qua Rash Tow*'. The 'little bundle of papers' contains an account of a visit to St Paul's Cathedral where the congregation bowed and curtsied to one another or slept instead of listening to the sermon. The papers also contain more general observations: 'The men of [England] are very cunning and ingenious ... but so very Idle, as to be carried up and down the streets in little covered Rooms by a Couple of Porters ... Their Dress is likewise very barbarous.' Addison claims that he was 'desirous of learning what Ideas they have conceived of us' and he uses the opportunity to poke fun at his own countrymen. But his conclusion carries a message of cultural relativism that is to be taken seriously.[3]

Addison's essay may be said to have pioneered one of the eighteenth century's most characteristic satirical tropes: the use of the innocent outsider to comment on the degeneracy of European culture.[4]

Irrespective of its stimulus for Addison's wit, the 1710 delegation was highly significant in its own right and deserves to be remembered. It came about largely in response to the struggle for control of the North American continent, itself a part of the global contest for empire that was conducted between Britain and

France during the first half of the eighteenth century. The Haudenosaunee were and are commonly referred to as the Iroquois, a name derived from their Huron/ Wyandot enemies, and meaning 'Bears'.[5] Their territory lay between the English settlements along the Eastern Seaboard of North America and the settlements of New France along the St Lawrence River and eastern Great Lakes areas. The Haudenosaunee (Iroquois) League comprised five main groups, Mohawk, Oneida, Onondaga, Cayuga and Seneca, and would be joined in 1722 by a sixth, the Tuscaroras. Each group had its own political, social and geographical position within a larger functional and symbolic habitation symbolised by the 'Longhouse' from which their collective name, Haudenosaunee, derived. The Seneca (in western New York State) occupied the western 'door' of the Longhouse, with the Cayuga, Onondaga, Oneida and Mohawk controlling successive territories eastward towards the Hudson River. At the easternmost 'door' of the Longhouse, the Mohawks, with their recently incorporated neighbours, the Mahicans, faced towards the European settlements bordering the Hudson: the Dutch and then, after the 1660s, the English.[6] Because geographically the Mohawk and Mahican were closest to the European settlements in New York, it is no surprise that representatives of these tribes comprised the 1710 delegation to London.

The turn of the century was a period of great change in the region, not least because of the growth of European colonial activities. The Haudenosaunee promoted an ideology of peace and conciliation to maintain their identities in this situation, sandwiched as they were between two mutually aggressive European powers.[7] Both the British and French colonial governments sought to make alliances with the Haudenosaunee at the very beginning of the eighteenth century and in this competitive context the People of the Longhouse tried to remain neutral, but their geographical location exposed them to constant diplomatic and military pressure.[8]

After an abortive attempt by the British to invade French Canada in 1709, the architects of that plan (Colonels Francis Nicholson, Samuel Vetch and especially Peter Schuyler) decided to bring over to England a number of Haudenosaunee headmen to conduct diplomatic negotiations for a further invasion attempt supported by the British Crown.[9] For their part, the Mohawk and Mahican delegates were concerned about the might of the French and hoped that more English missionaries might be sent to their lands, ostensibly to help in their conversion to Christianity and to counteract Jesuit influence.[10]

A contemporary account of the Indians' negotiating position, perhaps penned by Schuyler himself, is the *Four Indian Kings' Speech to Her Majesty* published by John Baker on 20 April 1710. Laced with Francophobe bias, the speech recounts the reasons for the visit of the Four Kings and the promise of their support in any military action that might be taken against French Canada. As reported in Baker's pamphlet, the Indian men

The true Effigies of the Four Indian Kings taken from the original paintings
After Simon Verelst, 20 April 1710
Engraving
342 x 266 mm (13¹/₂ x 10¹/₂")
The British Museum

Left to right
Sa Ga Yeath Qua Pieth Tow
88 x 68 mm (3¹/₂ x 2⁵/₈")

Ho Nee Yeath Taw No Row
88 x 70 mm (3¹/₂ x 2³/₄")

Bernard Lens III, 1710
Watercolour on ivory
The British Museum

… were mightily rejoiced when we heard by *Anadagarjaux* [Colonel Nicholson], that our Great Queen had resolved to send an Army to reduce Canada; from whose Mouth we readily embraced our Great Queen's Instructions; and in Token of our Friendship, we hung up the *Kettle*, and took up the *Hatchet*: … The Reduction of *Canada* is of such Weight, that after the effecting thereof, We should have *Free Hunting* and a great Trade with Our *Great Queen*'s Children: and as a Token of the Sincerity of the Six Nations, We do here, in the Name of All, present Our *Great Queen* with these BELTS of WAMPUM.[11]

For the interested parties at the Board of Trade and for the sponsors of this visit, this speech underlined the importance of the binding agreement being made between the English and the Haudenosaunee. For their part, in presenting belts of wampum, the People of the Longhouse were making an alliance that could not be broken unless the belts were returned.

The importance of the diplomacy with the Four Kings is also signalled in the number of official portraits made of them, with at least four separate

Etow Oh Koam
87 x 67 mm (3³/₈ x 2⁵/₈")

Tee Yee Neen Ho Ga Row
61 x 50 mm (2³/₈ x 2")

Bernard Lens III, 1710
Watercolour on ivory
The British Museum

**Tee Yee Neen Ho Ga Row,
Emperor of the Six Nations**
John Verelst, 1710
Oil on canvas
915 x 648 mm (36 x 25½")
Library and Archives, Canada,
acc. no. 1977-35-4. Acquired
with a special grant from the
Canadian Government, 1977

commissions at the time of their visit.[12] Of these, the small-sized full-length oil paintings by John Verelst are the most elaborate. Verelst came from an expatriate Dutch family of distinguished painters and was well regarded at court. He was paid the handsome sum of £100 for this commission and his completed Indian portraits hung in Kensington Palace during Queen Anne's lifetime.[13] These paintings were clearly intended to record a significant diplomatic meeting. The names of each of Verelst's sitters are known from John Simon's mezzotint engravings made after the originals, the only copies Verelst officially authorised.

**Sa Ga Yeath Qua Pieth Tow,
King of the Maquas**
John Verelst, 1710
Oil on canvas
915 x 645 mm (36 x 25⅜")
Library and Archives, Canada,
acc. no. 1977-35-2. Acquired
with a special grant from the
Canadian Government, 1977

Ho Nee Yeath Taw No Row,
King of the Generethgarich
John Verelst, 1710
Oil on canvas
915 x 651 mm (36 x 25⅝")
Library and Archives, Canada,
acc. no. 1977-35-3. Acquired
with a special grant from the
Canadian Government, 1977

The leader of the delegation, Theyanoguin, Hendrick
or Hendrick Peters is given the epithet Tee Yee Neen
Ho Ga Row, 'Emperor of the Six Nations'.[14] He is the
only man shown wearing a black frock coat, breeches
and silk stockings finished with buckled English
shoes.[15] His donning of English dress helps viewers
to locate his status as 'Emperor', ranking him with
the gentlemanly class of patrons and those colonial
officials with whom he had dealings in North
America. The other Indian men, Sa Ga Yeath Qua
Pieth Tow, 'King of the Maquas' (or Brant), Etow
Oh Koam, 'King of the River Nation' (or Nicholas)

Etow Oh Koam,
King of the River Nation
John Verelst, 1710
Oil on canvas
915 x 651 mm (36 x 25⅝")
Library and Archives, Canada,
acc. no. 1977-35-1. Acquired
with a special grant from the
Canadian Government, 1977

and Ho Nee Yeath Taw No Row, 'King of the Generethgarich' (or John) are more simply clothed in loose-fitting European-made white shirts belted around the waist with colourfully woven or decorated sashes. In the case of Etow Oh Koam this also serves as a holder for his sword, attached to the belt by further decorated loops.

Verelst's record of the delegation's clothing concurs with contemporary reports that they had been specially outfitted for their audience with the Queen and how, in addition, they were given red cloaks with gold braiding to wear over their garments.[16] But although they are portrayed wearing some English clothing, the Four Kings clearly exhibit signs of their own cultural identity and several objects that had been in their possession during their visit found their way into the cabinets of contemporary collectors (such as the warrior tie or burden strap shown here).[17] Theyanoguin, the so-called 'Emperor', hereafter referred to as Hendrick, also wears an

American Indian decorated belt or sash around his middle and proffers in his right hand a medium-sized and uniquely decorated wampum belt. The belt's design of crosses, picked out in white wampum shell beads against a dark-coloured beaded background, is significant for it may have been intended to indicate the delegation's interest in Christian missions, which in the minds of the colonisers made for more smoothly run and peaceable trading relations.[18] Wampum, made from the small white and purple shells of quahogs (hard clams) and whelks, was traded widely amongst eastern North American Indian groups. It has powerful properties as a mnemonic device and record of historical interchange and negotiation, and functioned both as symbol and contract in the diplomatic and negotiating policies of the Haudenosaunee, where traditionally it played a part in condolence rituals. Wampum also carries much sacred significance.[19] The belt shown in Verelst's portrait, with its cruciform patterns, would have registered as a symbol of allegiance and also of an affinity to Christian teachings.

Ironically, although a chapel was built in 1712 (since destroyed) at Fort Hunter, near present-day Albany, New York, modern leaders of the Haudenosaunee have revealed that this acceptance of Christian missionaries in the 1710s was not an act of submission. Instead, the Haudenosaunee valued missionaries primarily for their presumed ability to counteract witchcraft.[20]

Hendrick's companions are bare-legged and wear beaded moccasins of a type similar to a pair currently

Warrior tie or burden strap, tumpline
Hemp and moose hair
Length 500 mm (19⅝")
The British Museum

As shown worn around the waist in John Verelst's portraits of the Four Indian Kings.

held in the British Museum's Department of Ethnography.[21] Verelst was also concerned to record some of the symbolic skin markings of the delegation, clearly evident in the portraits and their mezzotint copies, such as the diagonal patterns of crossing black lines depicted on the face of the sitter known as Brant (Sa Ga Yeath Qua Pieth Tow), which indicates his participation in successful military expeditions against his enemies.[22] The figure of Nicholas (Etow Oh Koam) has several delicately painted images of thunderbirds tattooed across the right side of his face, both in Verelst's painting and in his portrait by Bernard Lens III from the set of ivory miniatures commissioned at the same time as Verelst's paintings. For many American Indian cultures thunderbirds were powerful sky spirits that could evoke the terrors and dangers of the natural world, an important spiritual support for any warrior.[23]

Hendrick was from the Mahicans, who had been adopted by the Mohawk, and his name in Mohawk, Theyanoguin, means 'He Who Lives a Double Life'.[24] The name is singularly apt, as it seems to anticipate his future role as a mediator between separate cultures and the dual aspect of his sympathies. Hendrick was also a Christianised Indian, probably from an early age, and eventually became a lay preacher for the Mohawks. The fact that he was an adoptee and also a believer in Christianity perhaps positioned him in an oblique relationship to the Haudenosaunee League as a whole. Certainly he would have been particularly sensitive to the need to understand cultural difference, whether Mohawk, Mahican or British. From the British point of view, of course, very little of this complexity could be understood. The delegation was presented as though comprising an emperor and three kings who were in positions of power over their people, as would be the case with European monarchs. The fact that the agreements reached in London held for any length of time back in America was entirely due to the skill of Hendrick and his companions in representing the British position to the League. However, the 'covenant chain' they forged in 1710 was at breaking point in the 1750s, on the eve of the Seven Years' War. Hendrick confronted the representatives of seven British colonies at the Albany Congress of 1754, declaring that 'the Governor of Virginia and the Governor of Canada are both quarrelling about lands which belong to Us, and such a quarrell as this may end in our destruction'.[25] He deplored the indecisiveness of the British in confronting the French but agreed to fight for the Crown. He lost his life at the Battle of Lake George in 1755.

In terms of its cultural impact, the responses in Britain to the 1710 visit ranged from elite to popular culture: from the detailed portrait likenesses made by John Verelst and Bernard Lens to the satirical accounts of such London wits as Joseph Addison and the production of printed materials (both in broadside and chapbook form) that recorded the Four Kings' presence in the capital. As late as 1800, following similar publications that had appeared throughout the eighteenth century, *The Garland of*

At Punch's Theatre.
For the Entertainment
of the Four Indian Kings
Printed book
Page 330 x 185 mm (13 x 7¼")
The British Library

33

The Garland of the Three Indian Kings
Published by J. Marshall, 1800?
Printed book
Page 105 x 55 mm (4⅛ x 2⅛")
The British Library

the Three Indian Kings repeated the tale of a romance that was supposed to have occurred between a British lady and one of the Kings, whose affections she had won. The woman's heart is moved when the King decides to convert to Christianity and denounce his uncouth ways. Although the narrative is invented, and the Indian Kings reduced in number from four to three, the *Garland* reveals that a dim echo of the 1710 embassy lingered in popular memory for almost a century.

Hendrick and his colleagues came to the court of Queen Anne on a serious mission to create lasting ties with the British, and within the court their political and military importance was properly recognised. Outside diplomatic circles, however, they were regarded more as sensational additions to the London scene, exotic specimens from an alien culture. The appellation 'Mohock' was applied in the 1710s to a group of aggressive young London socialites whose violent activities were likened by association to the '*Indian* Savages' of North America.[26]

This clash of interpretations is ultimately what is apparent in the portraits made of them, as Verelst and Lens wrestled with the problem of using European conventions to represent the unfamiliar world of the Four Kings. The combination of standard poses with signs of otherness is awkwardly presented, but this very awkwardness is itself revelatory of the way in which Hendrick and his companions challenged the preconceptions held about them.

NOTES

1 The most comprehensive account of the Mohawk and Mahican visit is Bond 1952. See also Garratt and Robertson 1985.

2 The performance took place on 24 April 1710. See Genest, *Some account of the English Stage, from the Restoration in 1660 to 1830*, Bath, 1832, vol. II, p. 451, cited in Bond 1952, pp. 4, 99.

3 Jonathan Swift claimed the idea was his: 'Yesterday [the *Spectator*] was made of a noble hint I gave him [Steele] long ago for his Tatler, about an Indian, supposed to write his travels into England. I repent he ever had it. I intended to have written a book on that subject. I believe he has spent it all in one paper.' Swift, *Journal to Stella*, 28 April 1711, printed as footnote 1 to the *Spectator*, no. 50 (27 April 1711), in Ross 1982, p. 558.

4 Bond (1952, p. 88) mentions later examples of this satirical trope. *Royal Remarks; or the Indian King's Observations On the most Fashionable Follies: Now reigning in the Kingdom of Great-Britain* appeared two decades after Addison's account in the *Spectator*. See also Pratt 1998.

5 For information on the accurate names of the 'Iroquois Nations', see www.sacred-texts.com/nam/iro/ibr/ibr16.htm and Hale 1883, app. A, note A: 'The Names of the Iroquois Nations'.

6 See Richter and Merrell 1987.

7 This is not to suggest that the period of early contact with Europeans was without war-making, but one must remember that the original creation of the League of the Haudenosaunee in the twelfth century had itself been inspired by both Hiawatha and Denigawidah's abhorrence of the violence that had previously existed inter-tribally within the separate nations. Nevertheless, ritual retaliation for losses in wartime was a constant factor in the behaviour of the Haudenosaunee towards others, and their reputation for this kind of devastating violence was built up amongst the colonising powers. For a discussion of the dating of the League of Haudenosaunee's formation and Denigawidah's conversion of Hiawatha to the path of peace, see Mann and Fields 1997.

8 For the Haudenosaunee historical relationships with their neighbours see Richter and Merrell 1987.

9 Bond 1952, pp. 19–21.

10 The historical accounts held in oral tradition by the elders of the Haudenosaunee indicate that the 1710 request for missionaries was initially made to combat the effect of 'witches' or negative influences in their local settlements, with the conversion to Christianity of secondary consideration. Keith Jamieson

(pers. comm.) at the Woodlands Cultural Center, Brantford, Ontario.

11 From the *Four Indian Kings' Speech to Her Majesty*, London, 1710. For the text of the speech as Baker printed it see Bond 1952, p. 94.

12 Bond (1952) mentions at least three different versions of their portraits taken from life: Verelst's paintings, Bernard Lens III's painted ivory miniatures and John Faber's bust-length mezzotints, a set of which is now held in the Newberry Library collections, D'Arcy McNickle Centre for the History of the American Indian, Chicago. Garratt (1985, p. 147) adds an additional set of watercolour portraits to those mentioned above. Bernard Lens Senior (II), father to Bernard Lens III, probably painted these after the miniatures on ivory by his son. These watercolours are in the Sloane manuscripts in the British Library, London (Add. MSS. 5253, fols 19–22). I would like to thank Kim Sloan at the British Museum for drawing my attention to these last examples.

13 Bond 1952, p. 66.

14 The description of 'Six Nations' here could not refer to the Tuscaroras, who would join the Haudenosaunee later, in 1722. It might refer instead to the Mahican delegate who, with his

allegiance to the Mohawk, would represent a sixth allied nation.

15 See 'Hendrick', *Dictionary of Canadian Biography*, at www.biogaphi.ca/EN/ShowBioPrintable.asp?BioId=35803.

16 Contemporary sources mention the adoption of English costumes by the delegation, one of them that Queen Anne herself gave them red cloaks decorated with gold braid. See Bond 1952 and Foreman 1943. E. Hinderaker (1996) considers Verelst's portraits to provide a newly conceived 'verbal and visual language of empire', which knitted disparate elements together to produce the idea of unity in diversity.

17 Sir Hans Sloane's collection of curiosities, which was incorporated in the founding of the British Museum in 1753, included American Indian items, three of which are derived from this 1710 delegation. Jonathan King has shown how the chronological basis for Sloane's catalogue strongly indicates that the numbers given to these items means that they entered his collection before the 1720s: see King 1994, p. 229. See also Turner 1955, pp. 50–60.

18 Keith Jamieson has suggested that the crosses could symbolise the number of missions or missionaries that would be allowed into the Mohawk territories.

19 Tehanetorens (Ray Fadden) 1999.

20 See note 10 above.

21 Jonathan King has drawn my attention to the close correspondence between a pair of moccasins decorated with quillwork and large glass beads, currently displayed in the British Museum, and those seen in Verelst's portraits. See King 1999, p. 57, fig. 51.

22 See Gilbert 2000, pp. 90–91.

23 Thunderbirds are discussed in Hultkrantz 1981.

24 See note 15 above.

25 Loc. cit.

26 The group were termed the 'Mohocks' or 'Mohock Club' and were accused of much drinking and harassing of innocent bystanders in early eighteenth-century London: see Addison's article in the *Spectator*, no. 324 (1712). Historians have recently questioned whether the Mohocks phenomenon was merely an invention in the minds of London's eighteenth-century urbanites: see Guthrie 1996.

2 William Ansah Sessarakoo

David Bindman

William Ansah Sessarakoo, the subject of Gabriel Mathias's 1749 portrait, was celebrated in mid-eighteenth-century England as a figure of romance. Though hailed as a 'prince', he was in fact the son of a wealthy slave-trader from West Africa who sent him on a grand tour of Europe with a companion, but they were both sold into slavery in Barbados by the captain of the ship taking them to England.[1] They were then ransomed by the Earl of Halifax, commissioner of trade and plantations, 'who gave orders for clothing and educating them in a very genteel manner'. Sessarakoo thus reached London as a celebrity and he and his companion were 'introduced to his majesty richly dressed, in the European manner, and were very graciously received'. Sessarakoo's high rank reminded Londoners of the popular story of *Oroonoko*, the subject of a novel by Mrs Aphra Behn and a much-performed play, which told the story of a noble African chief, a model of princely demeanour, 'who was betrayed by the treachery of a captain', and his tragic romance with the beautiful Imoinda. As it happens, *Oroonoko* was playing in London when Sessarakoo arrived and he was taken to a performance with his companion. It was reported that 'they were so affected, that the

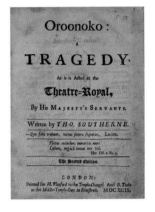

Oroonoko: A Tragedy
Thomas Southerne, 1699
Printed book
The British Library

William Ansah Sessarakoo, son of John Bannishee Carrante Chinnee of Anamaboe
Gabriel Mathias, 1749
Oil on canvas
666 x 558 mm (26¼ x 22")
The Menil Collection, Houston

Illustration to *Oroonoko*
Anon. after Henry Fuseli, c.1775
Engraving
167 x 113 mm (6⅝ x 4½")
The British Museum

tears flow'd plentifully from their eyes; the case of Oroonoko's being made a slave by the treachery of a captain being so very similar to their own'. Sessarakoo was so overcome that he left after the fourth act, while 'His companion remained, but wept the whole time; a circumstance which affected the audience yet more than the play, and doubled the tears that were shed for *Oroonoko* and *Imoinda*.'[2]

Sessarakoo was celebrated in a London journal
as 'A Young African Prince, Sold for a Slave', and
the treachery of the ship's captain who sold him
reminded people of another popular story of the
time, of the English trader Inkle, who ungratefully
sold his black mistress Yarico, who had rescued him
from attack, into slavery. Such visitors as Sessarakoo,
particularly if they were princes or of high status,
were especially welcome in London drawing rooms.
Their romantic aura differentiated them completely
from their less fortunate brethren, who were for
the most part slaves in domestic service and on the
plantations. The extended letterpress inscription
on the mezzotint print by John Faber after Gabriel
Mathias's painting makes much of the sitter's royal
ancestry. In the print as in the painting he is
presented as a gentleman in an elaborately brocaded
jacket with a hat under his left arm, a stance often
adopted by sea captains, perhaps as he was dressed
to meet the King. It is not clear whether he is wearing
a wig or his hair is combed into a wig-like shape;
nonetheless, it is very black and straight. The pose

William Ansah Sessarakoo
John Faber after
Gabriel Mathias, 1749
Mezzotint
559 x 406 mm (22 x 16")
The British Museum

Page from *Gentleman's*
Magazine
June 1750
National Portrait Gallery,
London

Job, Son of Solliman Dgiallo / of Bonda in the Country of Foota, Africa

Job, Son of Solliman Dgiallo
William Hoare, 1734
Etching
225 x 155 mm (8⁷/₈ x 6¹/₈")
The British Museum

and the brocade suggest a person of distinction, but hardly the figure of romance created, for example, by the poetic dialogues written by Thomas Dodd, a well-known popular writer of the day, and published in the *Gentleman's Magazine* in 1749.[5] There Sessarakoo is given a lover called Zara for whom he sighs in captivity, as Oroonoko sighed for Imoinda. Zara addresses his captors, emphasising the princely status of her lover: 'Hold, hold! Barbarians of the fiercest kind!/ … 'tis a prince ye bind;/ A prince, whom no indignities could hide/ They knew, presumptuous! And the Gods defy'd.'

   Sessarakoo was neither the first nor the last African to come to London in the eighteenth century as an honoured visitor, though he was the only one to be portrayed in an oil painting.[4] He was preceded by Job ben Solomon, who had a brief but well-reported stay in England in 1734, also after a period

Published according to Act of Parliament, Sept. 1, 1773 by Arch.ᵈ Bell, Bookfeller N.º 8 near the Saracens Head Aldgate.

of enslavement in Maryland. He was a devout Muslim from the Gambia who knew the Koran by heart and was able, after he had learned English, to render Sir Hans Sloane, the scholar and founder of the British Museum, great service in translating Arabic manuscripts. His portrait is known from the etched frontispiece, dated 1734, to his biography by his friend Thomas Bluett, the main source of information on his life and time in England.[5] It is signed and dated by 'Hoare' as painter and etcher, probably the well-known portraitist William Hoare.

Job lacks completely the traditional stereotype of African physiognomy that was already well established in art by the eighteenth century. Though his features are dark, he has a long, sharp nose, and wavy hair falling around his temples; neither his lips nor his nostrils are emphasised, as are Sessarakoo's. His exoticism is established by a turban and a gown,

Frontispiece to Phillis Wheatley's Poems
Scipio Moorhead, 1773
Engraving
559 x 406 mm (22 x 16")
The British Museum

and he carries a Koran held by a cord around his neck. As a Muslim he did not follow a religion completely unknown or completely alien to Christians. Yet he was regarded at this relatively early date as fully an African.

The next black celebrity to follow Sessarakoo in coming to Britain was the African-American poet Phillis Wheatley, author of *Poems on various subjects, religious and moral,* which she published at the age of nineteen in London in 1773. She was born in Africa and in 1761, at the age of seven, bought as a slave by a Boston family. Her literary gifts caused her to be separated by her owner from the other slaves, and her poems made her a celebrity in Boston, and then in London on her 1773 visit.[6] The frontispiece is a portrait of her after a design by a little-known black Boston artist, Scipio Moorhead,[7] though it was engraved in London. It is in the form of an oval, with around it the words: 'Phillis Wheatley, Negro Servant to Mr John Wheatley, of Boston'. She is presented according to the standard visual trope in British portraiture of 'the author', writing at a table, eyes raised and chin supported, as if dictating from heavenly inspiration. She has a demure face with large lips, conforming to the common European stereotype of Africans of the period, and emphasising the uniqueness at that time of someone of her background achieving the honour of having a book of poems published in London.

The rarity of this portrait as both of a famous black woman and by (as designer at least) an identifiable black artist might be taken as a sign of increasing black emancipation, and it belongs to the period of the earliest responses to the injustice of slavery in England. London reviewers were scathing of Wheatley's employer because the book's advertisement noted that she was still 'under the Disadvantage of serving as a Slave in a Family in this Town'. One reviewer, perhaps thinking of the evangelical spirit of her poems, was 'much concerned to find that this ingenious young woman is yet a slave',[8] suggesting that the provincial inhabitants of Boston were still unaffected by the now fashionable metropolitan distaste for slavery, following the Somerset case in the previous year, in which a runaway slave had been freed by the Court of King's Bench after a long-drawn-out and widely reported trial.

If Phillis Wheatley was an example of what was perceived increasingly in her time in England as the essential injustice of slavery, Sessarakoo had arrived, just twenty-four years earlier, when slavery was still fully accepted in England; it was only regarded as inappropriate for him because of his high social status. He thus lived a generation before the sea change in attitudes towards slavery that led to the foundation in 1787 by Granville Sharp and Thomas Clarkson of the Society for the Abolition of the Slave Trade and the abolition of the slave trade in Britain in 1807 and in the British colonies in 1833. Phillis Wheatley came to England at the beginning of the period when public opinion, for a whole variety of reasons, was turning against slavery, and she was one of the first beneficiaries of more benign attitudes to those of African descent.

NOTES

1 For a full account of Sessarakoo see Sypher 1941.

2 *The Gentleman's Magazine*, 19 (February 1749), p. 90.

3 Vol. 19 (July 1749), pp. 322–3: 'The African prince, now in England, to Zara at his father's court'; and August 1749, pp. 372–3: 'Zara, at the Court of Annamabboe, to the African Prince, now in England'.

4 There is a well-known portrait by Thomas Gainsborough of the African musician Ignatius Sancho but he lived all his adult life in England (see Phillips et al. 1997).

5 *Some Memoirs of the Life of Job, the Son of Solomon, the High Priest of Boonda in Africa, Who was a Slave about two years in Maryland; and afterwards being brought to England, was set free and sent to his native Land in the Year 1734*, London, 1735. There is also a modern biography of Job: Grant 1968.

6 For a full account of Wheatley see Kaplan and Kaplan 1989, pp. 170f.

7 For Scipio Moorhead, who was owned by the Rev. John Moorhead, and was the subject of one of Wheatley's poems, see op. cit. pp. 181–2.

8 Fryer 1984, p. 93.

OMAI a Native of UTAIETEA,

Brought into England in the Year 1774 by Tobias Furneaux Esq.r Commander of his Majesty's Sloop Adventure.
Humbly Inscribed to the Right Hon.ble JOHN EARL of SANDWICH, First Commissioner for executing
the OFFICE of Lord High Admiral of Great Britain and Ireland &c. &c.
By his Lordship's most devoted humble Servant,
Fra.s Bartolozzi

Publish'd according to Act of Parl.t 25th Oct.r 1774.

3 Mai

Jocelyn Hackforth-Jones

Each day, each week, each month has been a triumph.
The English in their mansions, in their salons and at
their tables have looked at him differently compared to
the English in their Great Cabins or on the beaches of
his island. Now their admiring, rather than domineering,
gaze gives him confidence …[1]

This imaginative reconstruction of the Tahitian Mai's reaction to the shifts in the behaviour of his English hosts and their 'admiring' rather than 'domineering' gaze strikingly positions Mai at the centre of his English 'triumph', where he is constantly aware of the admiration of society. During Captain James Cook's second voyage, Mai was able to persuade Captain Furneaux to let him board the *Adventure*. He arrived in London (ahead of Cook) on 14 July 1774.[2] In England he was called Omai, Omiah or Omy: O in Tahitian means 'it is', so Mai is closest to the Tahitian.

This chapter recounts the narrative of Mai's journey 'between worlds', and also shows that he had his own powerful reasons for travelling between worlds and for wishing to engage with English culture and people. It should be emphasised that Mai's agenda and his speaking voice are examined here from a European viewpoint, since our points of access

Omai (Mai), a native of Utaieta
Francisco Bartolozzi
after Nathaniel Dance, 1774
Engraving
461 x 291 mm (18 1/8 x 11 1/2")
The British Museum

are Western texts and paintings.

Immediately upon arriving in London in July 1774, Mai met Lord Sandwich, First Lord of the Admiralty, who in turn introduced him to Sir Joseph Banks and to the botanist Daniel Solander. Banks introduced Mai to London society, installed him in his London house, paid his bills and presented him at court. There were a number of favourable circumstances which may have contributed to his social success and to his emergence as a 'lyon' of society.[3] The educated public was already familiar with Jean-Jacques Rousseau's notion of the superiority of 'natural' man over 'civilised' man; more recently, the publication of two accounts of the Pacific (by Bougainville and Hawkesworth respectively) had made much of its

Omiah the Indian from Otaheite presented to their Majesties at Kew by Mr Banks & Dr Solander, July 17, 1774
Engraving
Plate mark 111 x 139 mm
(4⅜ x 5⅛")
National Library of Australia

OMIAH, the Indian from OTAHEITE, presented to their MAJESTIES at Kew, by Mr. Banks & Dr. Solander July 17. 1774.

sensuous delights and had taken the London reading public by storm. The climate was ripe for Mai's reception as (at the very least) the embodiment of 'natural man'. In fact, his formidable social skills were deployed to great effect. His sensitivity to individual social situations and his capacity for mimicking the manners and behaviour of his contemporaries, together with his considerable abilities as a performer, led to his participating in the London social round at the highest level. Three days after he had arrived, he was fitted with a maroon velvet coat, a white silk waistcoast and grey satin knee breeches and presented to the King and Queen at Kew by Sir Joseph Banks and Dr Solander. His bills indicate that his powerful patrons were content for him to have all

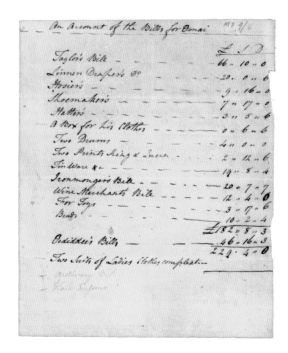

Mai's bill
Banks's papers
230 x 150 mm (9 x 5⁷/₈")
National Library of Australia

Mai's visiting card
Printed card
65 x 95 mm (2¹/₂ x 3³/₄")
Mark and Carolyn Blackburn,
Honolulu, Hawaii

the accoutrements of a gentleman, and he appears
to have spent lavishly on clothes, hats, shoes, wine
and servants – totalling many thousands of pounds
in today's terms. His elegant rococo visiting card
is another reminder of his gentlemanly status.
Contemporary written descriptions, such as that by
Fanny Burney (see below), describe in detail his court
attire. A more literal mark of the esteem in which
he was held, and the desire to keep him healthy, is
indicated by the King's recommendation that he
be inoculated against smallpox.[4] Here Banks and
Solander's ability to speak Tahitian helped in
communicating with Mai to allay any concerns about
the process.

Mai's own agenda was clear. He was aware that
he needed the support of key individuals in London
society to acquire material assistance and, most
crucially, firearms, in order to return to the South
Pacific and annihilate the Bora Borans, so that he
could lay claim to his native island of Raiatea.

He was born on the island of Raiatea in about
1753, probably into the middle class or *raatira*.[5] When
he was ten years old the island was attacked by the
Bora Borans and his father died in battle. Mai joined
numerous refugees fleeing to Tahiti, 100 miles to
the south-east, where they settled; he was still on
the nearby island of Huahine in 1773, at the time
of the brief visit of the *Resolution* and the *Adventure*
during Cook's second voyage. Having made friends
with some of the *Adventure*'s crew, he embarked as a
supernumerary, initially under the name of Tetuby
Homy. While apparently his English remained poor,

In Tahiti, white tapa was reserved for those of the highest or chiefly the status, *ari ´ i*. Thus Mai may have been using the process of sitting for this portrait as part of a strategy to (mis)-represent himself as belonging to a higher class.

Length of tapa cloth
Paper mulberry bark
2410 x 2250mm (94 7/8 x 88 5/8")
The British Museum

he became friendly with the officers on the *Resolution*, some of whom, like James Burney (brother of the diarist Fanny Burney), could converse with him in Tahitian.

His name was discovered later to have been a fabrication – his real name was Paridero, but he chose Mai since he wished to present himself as being of chiefly status and as a member of the noble or *ari'i* class.[6] Sir Joshua Reynolds's famous and impressive grand-scale portrait titled *Omai* of 1775–6 (see fig. 1 and the mezzotint illustrated here) on one level portrays the visual stereotype of Mai as noble savage.[7] The appearance and stiff texture of the white turban and the fabric of the flowing white robes have led to their identification as tapa or bark cloth.[8]

This visual stereotype persists: he is almost always portrayed in some type of 'native' dress, as in the Reynolds, or as a hybrid figure being presented at court shortly after his arrival in London – although in fact he always dressed in European dress during his sojourn in England.

In her letter to Samuel Crisp of 1 December 1774, Fanny Burney described her first meeting with her brother's Tahitian friend, a quiet, well-mannered figure who conveyed gentlemanliness without speaking:

I found Omai … He rose, & and made a very fine Bow & then seated himself again … When Mr Strange and Mr Hayes were Introduced to him, he paid his Compliments with great politeness to them, which he has found a method of doing without *words*.[9]

Omai (Mai)
Johann Jacobé
after Sir Joshua Reynolds
Published 1780
Mezzotint
544 x 330 mm (21 3/8 x 13")
National Portrait Gallery, London

The Mimic and
Model Gentleman

Mai is a great mimic, a cultural thespian. Good enough, anyway, to stop the superior sort of laughter that arises when he is not quite getting things right. He is mirror to his English hosts' civilities – courtesy, simplicity, carefulness. If he cannot read words on a page, he can read meanings in postures, status in things, gender and social relations in the spacings of a group.

Greg Dening

Burney's emphasis is fascinating, hinging as it does on the notion of gentlemanliness and politeness not needing words.[10] Clearly Mai here was not engaging in the art of conversation, but his gentlemanliness was a performance in which he used his entire body to suggest sensibility via gesture and expression, in addition to mastering how to stand, walk, sit and bow with great refinement. Given that Mai came from a culture that was primarily visual and oral rather than literary, it should not be surprising that he was quick to pick up and appropriate European visual codes. As Burney put it, 'He is tall & very well made … He makes *remarkably* good Bows – not for *him*, but for *any body*, however long under a Dancing Master's care.'[11]

Mai would have felt some affinity with the stratification, codes and rituals of London society since there were parallels with the hierarchical and ritualised nature of Tahitian society and the emphasis on dance and movement as integral to a range of ceremonies.[12] Burney suggested that Mai was in some respects superior to English gentlemen, with, as she put it, 'an understanding far superiour to the common race of *us cultivated gentry*'.[13] As she describes his exquisite gentility, there is almost the sense that Mai performs this better than an Englishman. One can only speculate whether it was not also an irritation for 'society' that this young man from Raiatea appeared so quickly and easily to master 'natural' codes of gentlemanliness which took his English counterparts many years to acquire, with the assistance of specialist training from dancing masters, tutors and the Grand Tour.[14]

Omai (Mai), a Polynesian
William Hodges, 1775–7
Oil on canvas
Framed 850 x 700 mm
(33 ½ x 27 ½ ")
Hunterian Museum at the Royal
College of Surgeons

Mai's grace of bearing was commented on with respect both to the Reynolds painting of him and to Nathaniel Dance's drawing, *Omai* of 1774 (where he is shown carrying his headrest), after which the engraving shown here is based (see p. 44).[15] Such portraits, together with William Parry's oil of *Omai (Mai), Sir Joseph Banks and Daniel Solander*, all reinforce the notion of his natural gentlemanliness and breeding. William Hodges also portrayed him in swathes of what appears once again to be white tapa cloth.[16]

It appears that Mai's efforts paid off and he was successful in gaining the support he needed. On 12 July 1776, nearly two years after he had arrived in England, Cook set off on his third voyage. His secret instructions stated: 'Upon your arrival at Otaheite … you are to land Omiah at such of them as he may chuse.'[17] Mai was given a number of objects with which to entertain his compatriots with descriptions of British life. These included miniature 'toys', such as soldiers, animals and coaches; a barrel organ; portraits of the King and Queen; an illustrated bible; a jack-in-the-box; globes, maps and charts; drums; an electrical machine; clothes; cooking

Headrest or stool
Wood, 150 x 440 x 200 mm
(5 ⅞ x 17 ⅜ x 7 ⅞ ")
The British Museum

Omai (Mai), Sir Joseph Banks and Daniel Solander
William Parry, 1775–6
Oil on canvas
1525 x 1525 mm (60 x 60")
National Portrait Gallery, London

Here Mai is shown with two key players in South Seas scientific exploration, namely Sir Joseph Banks and the Swedish scientist Dr Daniel Solander. Both men had accompanied Cook on his first voyage. The painting strikingly suggests the notion of these non-European visitors caught 'between worlds' and focuses on relationships forged across cultural boundaries.

Mai is shown in white robes similar to those in the Reynolds mezzotint and which may in fact be white tapa (bark), indicating the other performance in which he engaged: representing himself as coming from the noble or *ari'i* class.

A human sacrifice in a Morai
in Otaheite
William Woollett, 1784
Engraving
Plate mark 290 x 490 mm
(11³/₈ x 19¹/₄")
National Library of Australia

Mai can be seen in naval uniform
in the far right foreground.

utensils; and, perhaps most significantly and importantly for Mai, guns, powder and shot. He was later strikingly (if fancifully) represented in one engraving arriving in Tahiti as a triumphal European chivalric leader, dressed in armour and riding beside Cook, his firearms blazing, a personification of European power and prestige.

When he first encountered Mai in 1774, Cook had been unimpressed, describing him as 'dark, ugly and a downright blackguard'.[18] But by 1776 he had unequivocally reversed his opinion, both of Mai's character and of his skills as an interpreter. This is substantiated in a series of fascinating engravings of Mai after paintings by John Webber and illustrations to other accounts of the third voyage, showing him, for example, in British naval uniform acting as a mediator, as in the engraving of *A human sacrifice in a Morai, in Otaheite* of 1784. Here Cook, Anderson and Mai stand on the right, observing the sacrifice in the centre. According to Cook's journal, Mai expressed the Europeans' revulsion, presumably with the aim of gaining the support of his powerful British friends by acting as an intermediary or, as Cook would have

Omai's Public Entry on his first
landing at Otaheite
From Rickman's *Journal of
Captain Cook's Last Voyage*, 1781
Printed book
Page 170 x 100 mm (6³/₄ x 3⁷/₈")
The British Library

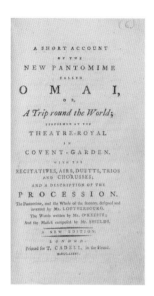

Omai, or, A Trip round the World
1785
Printed playbill
230 x 180 mm (9 x 7⅛")
The British Library

it, 'Omai was our spokesman and entered into our arguments with so much spirit that he put the Cheif [*sic*] out of all manner of patience.'[19]

Just as when Mai arrived in London, when he returned to Tahiti in August 1777 and encountered his own people, it is clear from written accounts that he engaged in a double mimicry, not just imitating English gentlemanliness but also assuming a position that he did not actually occupy in his own culture. As one of Cook's officers put it:

poor Omai was of so little consequence here as not to be known, we found that Omai was an assum'd name, his real name being Parridero; Captain Cook asked him why he had taken the former name in preference to his own, he reply'd that ... he thought to pass for a great Man ....[20]

Mai appeared to be strategically using his encounter with Europe to elevate his own position at home. He was quick to see that the acquisition of guns and other European commodities would give him a superior status back in Tahiti, where he was unable to pretend that he came from the noble *ari'i* class. Cook commented that both the chief and Mai's own family seemed indifferent to him until he presented them with gifts.[21]

In England, contemporary visual and literary representations had described Mai's many social and personal skills: his charm, humour, wit, grace and ease of bearing. His ability to impress those he met and to capture the public imagination is reflected in the staging of John Keefe's remarkable 'adult pantomime', *Omai, or, a Trip round the World* in 1785, some eight years after Mai had left England. His celebrity status and the continuing popular fascination with the exotic were further highlighted by the success of the pantomime – the performance was repeated fifty times during the season – although this also had much to do with the inventiveness of Philip de Loutherbourg's sets and extraordinary special effects, which included whirlpools, volcanoes and shipwrecks.[22] The playbill once again repeats the misperception that Mai was of royal blood.

Unlike many indigenous visitors to England during the eighteenth century, Mai was never really paraded as an exotic specimen, nor was he given a useful trade or literary education; rather, he successfully took on the role of a gentleman and an aristocrat between worlds, engaging in a strategic mimicry for his own ends.[23]

Scene from *Omai, or,*
A Trip round the World
Philip de Loutherbourg, 1785
Paper model
Approx. 400 x 600 x 400 mm
(15³⁄₄ x 23⁵⁄₈ x 15³⁄₄")
V&A Museum of Performance

NOTES

1 Dening 2001, pp. 53–4.

2 McCormick 1977, p. 94.

3 Many of Mai's European contemporaries, including Fanny Burney, noted that he was lionised by society.

4 Connaughton 2005, pp. 118ff.

5 See Tarlton and McCormick 1977, p. 11.

6 Beaglehole (ed.) 1967, p. 1343.

7 See also Guest 1992.

8 Turner 2001, pp. 23–30.

9 Letter to Samuel Crisp, 1 December 1774, in Troide et al. (eds) 1958, p. 601.

10 See Klein 1994.

11 Letter to Samuel Crisp, 1 December 1774, in Troide et al. (eds) 1958, p. 601.

12 'So far from being an unsophisticated "savage", an untaught man of "nature" he was the product of a settled and relatively complex manner of life', Tarlton and McCormick 1977, p. 12.

13 Letter to Samuel Crisp, 1 December 1774, in Troide et al. (eds) 1958, p. 62.

14 For an extended analysis of Mai's agendas see Hackforth-Jones 2006.

15 This headrest was recently purchased by the Bishop Museum in Hawai for £80,000 sterling.

16 For an account of this painting see also Smith (1960) 1989.

17 McCormick 1977, p. 187.

18 Beaglehole (ed.) 1967, p. 428.

19 Op. cit., pp. 197–9.

20 Op. cit., p. 1343.

21 J. Cook, *A Voyage to the Pacific Ocean undertaken by the command of his Majesty, for making Discoveries in the Northern Hemisphere …in 3 vols. Vols I and II written by Capt. James Cook,* London, 1784, vol. 2, p. 9.

22 Smith (1960) 1989, pp. 115ff.

23 See Thomas 1991. Thomas's notion of cultural entanglement is helpful, particularly in his suggestion that 'in certain phases of … colonial history, indigenous peoples are no less powerful and no less able to appropriate than the whites'.

Thayeadanegea,
Joseph Brant
the Mohawk Chief.

4 Joseph Brant (Thayendanegea)

Stephanie Pratt

Joseph Brant, or Thayendanegea to use his Mohawk name, was perhaps the most accomplished and well-received North American Indian visitor to England during the eighteenth century. His two visits to Britain, one in 1775–6 and the other in 1785–6, were undertaken to reaffirm alliances with the English at the time of the American Revolution and to gain assurances from colonial administrators and the British Crown that their promises of protection would not be forgotten once the American campaigns had been concluded.[1] Brant was a protégé of Sir William Johnson (1715?–1774), first superintendent of Indian Affairs for the Northern Department in North America.[2] Brant's sister was Johnson's common-law wife and Johnson supported Brant's education.[3] He was sent to Moor's Charity School in Lebanon, Connecticut, run by the Reverend Eleazor Wheelock, where he learned to speak and write fluent English and converted to Christianity. In 1786 Brant published his own translation of the Gospel of St Mark into the Mohawk language.

Brant's predecessors in Mohawk diplomacy, the 'Four Indian Kings' of the 1710 delegation, had created both a social and a diplomatic stir, but the preconception of American Indians as uncivilised

Gospel of St Mark in English and Mohawk, translated by Joseph Brant
Published by C. Buckton, 1787
Printed book
Page 220 x 140 mm (8 ⅝ x 5 ½")
The British Library

The Mohawk language title page is illustrated.

Joseph Brant (Thayendanegea)
George Romney, 1776
Oil on canvas
1270 x 1016 mm (50 x 40")
National Gallery of Canada, Ottawa. Transfer from the Canadian War Memorials, 1921

Brant's Masonic apron
1776
Silk, leather, silver metallic threads
318 x 368 x 50 mm
(12½ x 14½ x 2")
Barton Lodge
A.F. & A.M. #6 G.R.C., Hamilton,
Ontario, Canada

savages proved hard to dislodge.[4] Joseph Brant, emerging as a war leader in quite different circumstances to those of his predecessors, did everything he could to dispel the perception of 'Mohawk' and 'American Indian' as synonymous with uncouth and unreasonable behaviour. In 1761 he had shown himself to be a loyal ally in several of the battles in America that had taken place as part of the Seven Years' War of 1754–61.[5] In the 1770s he attained the rank of Captain in the British Army, and while he was in England he was adopted into a Masonic lodge and befriended by such members of the social elite as James Boswell and Hugh Percy, 2nd Duke of Northumberland.[6]

Boswell made a point of meeting Brant during his first trip to England, visiting him in his quarters in Lad Lane and writing a description of him for the *London Magazine* of July 1776:

This chief had not the ferocious dignity of a savage leader;
nor does he discover any extraordinary force of either mind
or body … a print of him in the dress of his nation gives
him a more striking appearance; for when he wore the
ordinary European habit, there did not seem to be any
thing about him that marked pre-eminence … His manners
are gentle and quiet, and to those who study human nature,
he affords a very convincing proof of the tameness which
education can produce upon the wildest race.[7]

Boswell's puzzlement over the location of Brant's
identity was heightened by his tendency to appear in
'European dress, [for] there was nothing besides his
colour to mark wherein he differed from other men'.[8]
The adoption of European attire seems to have been
a deliberate strategy by such important cultural
brokers and go-betweens as Brant, and other
sachems before him.[9] Poised as an intermediary, he
maintained his allegiance to his own people, their
beliefs and customs and safeguarded their interests;
but he was able to captivate the English and to gain
their trust and support on the strength of his
personal qualities, his behaviour and his appearance.

Contemporary portraits of Brant show him in
costumes combining elements of Mohawk
significance, such as the feathered headdress, shell
gorget and other American Indian crafted items, with
emblems of his association with the British, such as
the English-made silver gorget (a personal gift from
King George III), linen shirt, Masonic cross and silver
brooches created for the 'Indian trade'. This style of
dress, hybridising European and Indian elements, had

Joseph Brant's gorget
1776
Silver, 102 x 102 mm (4 x 4")
Joseph Brant Museum,
Burlington, Ontario, Canada

It is noteworthy that Brant's
portraits show him in
hybridised costume, very
different to his purely
European dress described
by observers in London.

become a feature of the American frontier and, in a
sense, spoke for the new identities being created in
the 'middle ground' between Indian communities and
European colonists.[10]

Brant sat for his portrait twice on his first visit to
London. James Boswell arranged for a now unknown
artist to make a pencil drawing of the Mohawk leader
to accompany his account in the *London Magazine*
for July 1776. Although this would have ensured
a wide circulation of Brant's image, the more
prestigious likeness was the three-quarter-length
portrait painted by George Romney, for which Brant
posed on 29 March and again on 4 April 1776. The
portrait was commissioned by the Earl of Warwick,
and hung in Warwick Castle for many years.[11] An
engraving derived from this portrait was later used as
the frontispiece to William Leete Stone's *Life of Joseph
Brant* (1838). Brant greatly approved of this likeness
and was himself presented with a box of engravings
taken from it.[12]

Joseph Brant (Thayendanegea)
John Raphael Smith
after George Romney, 1776
Mezzotint
686 x 508 mm (27 x 20")
The British Museum

JOSEPH TAYADANEEGA called the BRANT,

the Great Captain of the Six Nations.

Engraved from an Original Painting of G. Romney in the Collection of the Right Hon.ble the Earl of Warwick by J.R.Smith.

Published as the Act directs 1.st Feb.y 1779.

The fact that one of the leading artists of the
time was employed to make such a dignified portrait
speaks of the seriousness with which the British
viewed their Indian allies at the outbreak of the
American Revolution in 1775. Not all the Mohawk
had promised allegiance to England, and on his
return to America Brant did his utmost to persuade
those with whom he had some influence to join the
Loyalists. His importance was not merely diplomatic,
however: a pipe-tomahawk, another item designed
for the Indian trade, is shown in his right hand to
emphasise his military prowess. An alliance with this
commander of irregular troops was greatly to be
valued, for it was rumoured that he could bring
three thousand warriors into the field.[13] General
Haldimand, Commander-in-Chief of all Canada
during the Revolutionary War, noted with approval
Brant's leadership and his commitment to the British
cause, stating that the military successes of the
Rangers and the Indian auxiliaries in 1778 'Must be
Attributed greatly to the Indian Joseph Briant [sic]
Whose Attachment to Government, resolution And
Personal Exertion, makes him a character of a very
distinguished Kind'.[14]

Brant's second mission to England, in 1785–6,
was undertaken after the Treaty of Paris had been
signed in 1783 between the newly formed United
States government and the British.[15] There were no
American Indian delegates at the peace talks and the
British negotiators failed to represent their tribal
allies. Many of the American Indian peoples who had
made common cause with the Loyalist side found
themselves expropriated of their lands in what were

now territories controlled by the United States. Shortly after the signing of the peace treaty Brant made a speech in Quebec to General Haldimand, reminding him of the long-standing alliance between his people and the Crown, 'our Allies for whom We have often so freely bled'.[16]

His main reason for travelling to Britain in the 1780s was to reinforce his claims for compensation and to arrange for his Mohawk people to be resettled in lands designated for them in the province of Upper Canada, alongside the Grand River in what is now Ontario. He also succeeded in arranging a lifetime pension for himself.

Brant still attracted interest in Britain, even though the cause he represented was lost. The American artist Gilbert Stuart was working in London at the time, under the tutelage of his compatriot, Benjamin West.[17] Stuart received two commissions to make Brant's likeness. In the version commissioned by Hugh Percy, 2nd Duke of Northumberland (Syon House, London), the youthful Brant of Romney's idealised portrait has been replaced by a middle-aged man of 43, his face thinner, his features drawn, as though manifesting his anxieties for the future of his people. The Duke of Northumberland was a firm friend of Brant: both men had served in the British forces stationed near Boston during the Revolutionary Wars, and Northumberland had been adopted by the Mohawks and given the name Thorighwegeri, meaning 'the Evergreen Brake'.[18] They maintained a correspondence up until Brant's death and it was the Duke who commissioned a

presentation pipe-tomahawk to be awarded to the
Mohawk leader on his planned third visit in 1807;
however, Brant died in November 1807, still in
Canada, before the gift could be presented.[19]

Another of Brant's friends from his military days,
Francis Rawdon-Hastings, the Earl of Moira,
commissioned the second portrait of Brant by Gilbert
Stuart.[20] In this image Brant is rather more idealised
and shown in a twisting pose, looking to his left, his
head tilted slightly upwards. His dress is more simply
arranged than in his other portraits, with emphasis
given to the native-designed shell gorget at his neck
and the fur-lined and striped trade blanket draped
across his left shoulder. His feather headdress is
shown more fulsomely displayed in all its colour and
distinctiveness. The sweeping clouds trailing behind
create the feeling that Brant is still the inspired war
leader and orator he had always been. Stuart's two
paintings capture different facets of Brant's
personality, but for all their differences of mood
the Moira and Northumberland portraits are both
essentially romanticised, even elegiac memorials
to a man and a situation whose time was passing.

Perhaps even more than his probable great-
grandfather, Hendrick (Theyanoguin) of the 1710
delegation, Joseph Brant can be seen as straddling
the separate worlds of which he was a part. Like
Hendrick, Brant was not a member of the Mohawk
by birth, being Wyandot or Huron on his father's
side. As with Hendrick, this oblique relationship to
the Haudenosaunee League perhaps allowed him
to operate more successfully on and beyond the

Joseph Brant (Thayendanegea)
also known as The Moira Portrait
Gilbert Stuart, 1786
Oil on canvas
762 x 610 mm (30 x 24")
The British Museum

frontier in the late eighteenth century. The conflict for North America threw settled identities into crisis, literally redrawing the map as territorial control passed from Indians first to European colonists and then to the new United States. In a kaleidoscopic world of shifting allegiances, the successful leader was one who understood how the relationship between an individual, a people and a land had to be reinterpreted and renegotiated if it was not to be destroyed. Brant is a particularly interesting example of this phenomenon, given his consummate ability to renegotiate his identity to suit new circumstances. Thayendanegea, his Mohawk name, means 'He Who Sets or Places Together Two Bets', which suggests an ability to offset possible loss through strategic foresight. His differing reputations bear witness to his success in this: in the United States he was the 'monster Brandt [sic]' who was (wrongly) blamed for the Wyoming Valley massacre of 1778. For some of the Iroquois, especially those who fought on the side of the United States, he was seen as the great betrayer who had sold off tribal lands to speculators for his own personal profit. In Canada, however, he was regarded as a responsible leader and representative of his people, who safeguarded their interests through a period of cultural change. And in Britain he was the loyal ally and friend who could guarantee tribal support for George III and his war against the American rebels. The portraits made of Brant can be considered, to this extent, as deliberately reinforcing the image he wished to project to his British allies.

NOTES

1 See Thompson Kelsay 1984. Brant told James Boswell he was descended from one of the Mohawk men who had visited London in 1710. See Scott and Pottle 1928–34, vol. 11, p. 257 (cited by Thompson Kelsay, p. 14). Although many sources link him to Brant (Sa Ga Yeath Qua Pieth Tow) of the 1710 delegation, this is not universally accepted. One of Joseph Brant's descendants claimed that his mother was Hendrick's granddaughter; see 'Thayendanegea' in *Dictionary of Canadian Biography* (www.biograph.ca/EN/ShowBio Printable.asp?BioId=360808).

2 See O'Toole 2005.

3 Molly Brant acted as an important cultural mediator in her own right.

4 See Pratt 2005.

5 He is reported to have been present at the Battle of Lake George in 1755 aged thirteen, under the protection of William Johnson, the Indian agent. Brant

also took part in Abercromby's campaign (1758), William Johnson's expedition against Fort Niagara (1759) and Jeffery Amherst's siege of Montreal (1760).

6 See Thompson Kelsay 1984, pp. 165–71 for Brant's successes in London.

7 Cited in Hamilton 1958, p. 121.

8 Quoted from Foreman 1943, p. 94. See also Reinhardt 1998, pp. 283–305.

9 The term 'sachem' signifies a civil chief representing his clan in Haudenosaunee League councils. Brant did not inherit this title from his mother, as would have been customary for *sachems* of the Haudenosaunee. He, did, however act in such a capacity after the American Revolutionary War, when he became the recognised leader of those Mohawks who followed him to the Grand River settlement in present-day Ontario. See Thompson Kelsay 1984, pp. 38–41, 350.

10 Thompson Kelsay (1984, p. 536) mentions episodes later in his life when Brant was observed changing his dress to present a more 'Indian' fashion when travelling out to the frontier settlements and into Indian country. See also Shannon 1996, pp. 13–42.

11 Fawcett Thompson 1969, pp. 49–53.

12 Thompson Kelsay 1984, p. 169.

13 The figure of 3,000 warriors is reported by Boswell in his notice of Brant and the Mohawks, printed in the *London Magazine* of July 1776 (cited in Thompson Kelsay 1984, p. 172). Kelsay speculates that Boswell must have been given this information either by Captain Gilbert Tice, who accompanied Brant to London, or by Brant himself.

14 Thompson Kelsay 1984, p. 167.

15 Brant's argument for adequate resettlement in British-controlled territory is part of a broader

picture following the Revolutionary War, when the British attempted to retain their frontier forts, such as Detroit, allying with Indian groups to resist US expansion into the 'Old Northwest'.

16 State Papers Canada, Q21: 236–42.

17 Barratt and Miles 2004, pp. 25–9.

18 Op. cit. p. 70.

19 My thanks to Jonathan King of the British Museum's Centre for Anthropology for drawing my attention to this final intended visit.

20 The original painting by Stuart is now in the Fenimore Museum, Cooperstown, NY. The provenance of the British Museum's almost identical version is obscure, but it was in the department of Ethnology from the early decades of the twentieth century.

Native name Ben-nel-long

5 Bennelong & Yemmerrawanne

Jocelyn Hackforth-Jones

The noise of the Men, Crying and screaming of the Women & Children together with the situation of the two miserable wretches in our possession was really a most distressing scene … it was by far the most unpleasant service I ever was order'd to execute. These People were shaved, wash'd and cloathed; an Iron shackle was put on one leg with a rope made fast to it and a Convict charged with each of them, they were very sullen & sulky…[1]

This eyewitness account describes the forcible removal from Sydney, New South Wales, of Bennelong and his companion Colby nearly two years after British settlement in January 1788. The passage, taken from the diary of William Bradley, First Lieutenant on the HMS *Sirius*,[2] records not only the capture of the two indigenous inhabitants, Woollarawarre Bennelong and Colby on 25 November 1789, but also their return to Government House and their consequent shackling to prevent escape. In the watercolour accompanying Bradley's journal, the Bush itself becomes a metaphor for danger: in the centre of the bay, officers are carrying their captives to the boat, while local Eora people advance with spears on either side.[3] The numerous texts describing the relationship between the Governor of the colony and Bennelong

Bennelong

Inscribed: Native name Ben-nel-long. As painted when angry after Botany Bay Colebee was wounded
Port Jackson painter, 1790
Work on paper
203 x 173 mm (8 x 6³/₄")
The Natural History Museum, London

**The Taking of Colbee
and Benallon [*sic*],
25 November 1789**
William Bradley, 1789
Watercolour
165 x 230 mm (6½ x 9")
Mitchell Library, State Library
of New South Wales

The watercolour shows armed British troops carrying their
captives to the boat while local Eora men with spears
advance on either side of the bay. It is a powerful reminder
of the numbers of indigenous people who were taken against
their will.

include, most notably, the diaries and journals of the officers of the First Fleet who, under the command of Governor Phillip, had established the first penal settlement in New South Wales. Many of these accounts were later published.[4]

More peaceful attempts to persuade the local Aboriginal people to interact with the Europeans had been unsuccessful, so (according to Bradley) the Governor judged it necessary to take them by force. His expressed intention was to learn about their customs and language: in his dispatches he had already lamented his failure to 'open an intercourse' with the indigenous people as instructed by the King.[5] The initial purpose behind the capture of Bennelong and Colby was so that they might serve as ethnographic specimens. Governor Phillip also wanted intermediaries who would learn English and thus be equipped to give the settlers information about the local indigenous inhabitants.

Colby escaped after a few days, but Bennelong remained in captivity for some six months before he also made a successful bid for freedom. Bennelong's sojourn in Government House had earned him the approbation of the British, who noted that he conducted himself with the 'greatest propriety at table', particularly when ladies were present, and that his 'dress appeared to be no small concern with him'.[6] As an Eora man, Bennelong would have been acutely aware of his appearance as a marker of social occasion. After his escape he continued to maintain cordial contact with Governor Phillip, despite an unfortunate episode in September 1790 when he orchestrated a meeting with the Governor at Manly Beach. Following what was generally represented as a 'misunderstanding', one of Bennelong's companions speared Governor Phillip in the shoulder using Bennelong's hooked spear. A few days later, Bennelong called at Government House to enquire after the Governor's health and to apologise. More recently, writers have suggested that this was a ritual punishment orchestrated by Bennelong in order to punish the Governor for his kidnapping and imprisonment.[7] This was very much part of Bennelong's culture: it does not necessarily indicate a 'change' in his cordial behaviour towards the Governor, but simply his belief that the Governor also needed to be punished for his treatment of Bennelong and Colby.

On 10 December 1792, nearly three years after he was first captured by force, Bennelong (then approximately twenty-eight years old) and his teenage companion, Yemmerrawanne,[8] became the first Australian Aborigines to leave the colony of New South Wales bound for England aboard the ship *Atlantic*. By this time Bennelong had established a reputation for himself as a skilled intermediary between the British and his own people, the Eora of the coastal region of Sydney. He was described as intelligent and humorous, and acknowledged by at least one of Phillip's officers to be a reliable go-between. He was also a clever mimic, capable of imitating the reactions and gestures of every member of the Governor's family.

During the six months that Bennelong lived in

P. Neagle Sc.

captivity at Government House he had attempted to introduce Phillip to the complex web of relationships that comprise Aboriginal kinship systems. It appears, too, that he was a canny politician and a proficient intercultural negotiator. That he was also a powerful and proud warrior is clear from contemporary accounts and the watercolour *Native Name Ben-nel-long. As painted when angry after Botany Bay Colebee* [sic] *was wounded* (p. 68). The blazing anger represented in the latter is striking since it is more forceful than contemporary conventions for the representation of

Portrait of Bennelong in
An Account of the English Colony of New South Wales
David Collins, 1798
Work on paper
135 x 210 mm (5¼ x 8¼")
The Natural History Museum, London

Yemmerrawanne
Artist and date unknown
Pen and wash on light board
95 x 65 mm (3³/₄ x 2¹/₂")
Dixson Library State Library
of New South Wales

indigenous peoples of the South Pacific. These were more distanced ethnographic representations and generally portrayed Aboriginal people going about their daily activities.[9] By the 1790s both French and British representations of native peoples had moved away from invoking such idealising conventions associated with the noble savage, as epitomised by Reynolds's portrait of *Omai* (see p. 10), towards a greater concern for more realistic representation.[10]

After arriving in England on 22 May 1793, Bennelong and Yemmerrawanne were outfitted by London tailors Knox and Wilson with frock coats, knee breeches, striped waistbands and spotted waistcoats. They lodged at the home of William Waterhouse in Mount Street, Mayfair.[11] Governor Phillip presented them at court in St James's Palace. Contemporary written records, like the visual references, remain fragmentary, but offer us occasional glimpses of the two men being taken to see the sights, or observed 'at a window in St James's Street, to see the company going to St James's', where they were observed as part of the spectacle of court culture.[12] One wonders how the two men responded to a trip to the Theatre Royal, Covent Garden;[13]

Bennelong
Artist and date unknown
(William Waterhouse?)
Pen and wash on light board
95 x 65 mm (3³/₄ x 2¹/₂")
Dixson Library State Library
of New South Wales

they were also taken swimming, and sightseeing to
St Paul's, Westminster, and to the Tower of London,
attended by servants. A small contemporary
miniature, probably by William Waterhouse (W.W.)
shows Bennelong as a soberly and well-dressed
gentleman sporting brushed curls and a spotted
waistcoat. The collar in the tiny silhouette of
Yemmerrawanne also points to gentlemanly dress.

According to David Collins, the Judge Advocate,
while both men had undertaken the voyage to
England on a voluntary basis, upon arrival they
were anxious to return to their homeland, saying
that their wives expected them back within the year.[14]
Unlike Mai, who swiftly became a celebrity figure and
appears from the start to have been engaged in a
strategic process, Bennelong and Yemmerrawanne
had no clear motives for leaving New South Wales.
Governor Phillip undoubtedly exerted strong pressure
and inducements in his desire to display them back
in England, and he may have made promises that
he never delivered. I would also speculate that
Bennelong may have felt that it behoved him to
accompany Phillip to London, since they were in a
kinship relationship.

On arriving in London Bennelong and Yemmerrawanne were likely to have been negatively regarded as ethnographic specimens from a colony (New South Wales) that had recently been established as a distant penal colony for British convicts.[15]

The notion of Bennelong moving between worlds is visually encapsulated most effectively in an engraved portrait after a drawing by David Collins, published in his *An Account of the English Colony of New South Wales* in 1798, where he is depicted as a gentleman juxtaposed against an assemblage of Aboriginal weaponry (see p. 73). The central cartouche is based on the miniature of Bennelong described above. Behind this are weapons, including the local Eora long fighting spears with ridges at the ends, similar to the pointed spear used to pierce Governor Phillip some months earlier, at his meeting with Bennelong at Manly Beach.[16]

The process of travelling between worlds and settling in England undermined the health of both visitors: both suffered as a result of the comparative damp and cold of the English climate. Yemmerrawanne died in London on 18 May 1794, while Bennelong returned home in 1795 with Governor Hunter, the newly appointed Governor of New South Wales.

Accounts of Bennelong have frequently regarded him as a doomed victim of contact with Europeans, and according to many contemporary accounts he was one of the first to engender the stereotype of the drunken Aborigine. This, too, seems to be a misrepresentation. Recent revisionary accounts have analysed the myriad of colonial sources and invoked concepts of Australian Aboriginal kinship to gain a better understanding of the man and his agenda. The notion of the drunken Aborigine at this time is largely a colonial construction and refers to the period after Bennelong returned to Sydney. What is beyond doubt is that Bennelong's character was far more complex than has been previously thought and that, like Mai before him, he also had his own personal reasons and agendas for interacting with Europeans.[17]

NOTES

1 W. Bradley, 'A Voyage to New South Wales', December 1786–May 1792, manuscript in Mitchell Library, Sydney, New South Wales: entry for 25 November 1789.

2 HMS *Sirius* was the flagship of the First Fleet which established the penal colony in New South Wales in 1788.

3 For related imagery where the Bush is also represented as a metaphor for danger see Smith and Wheeler 1988, p. 66.

4 Some are quoted directly in this essay but for a fuller account and further references see Brodsky 1973; K.V. Smith 2001. The most accessible account of the watercolours and contemporary narratives is Challis 2000.

5 See Kenny 1973, p. 6.

6 Collins (1798) 1975, p. 367.

7 See K.V. Smith 2001, pp. 57–9

for a re-examination of the evidence.

8 Also spelled Yemmerawannie.

9 See also K.V. Smith 2001, p. 89.

10 See particularly B. Smith (1960), 1989.

11 Smith, Bourke and Riley 2006. I am indebted to K.V. Smith's work on this subject.

12 Brodsky 1973, p. 65.

13 Mitchell Library catalogue entry under Yemmerrawanne.

14 Collins (1798) 1975, p. 296.

15 'The natural curiosities aroused the interest of the British public far more than the story of the foundation of the penal settlement', K.V. Smith 2001, p. 162.

16 Op. cit., pp. 57–9.

17 Loc. cit.

Drawn on Stone from the life by T.M.Baynes.

Printed by C.Hullmandel.

SAKE DEEN MAHOMED.
SHAMPOOING SURGEON.
BRIGHTON.

Publ.d by the Artist 41.Burton Street, Burton Crescent.

6 Sake Dean Mahomed

Romita Ray

Sake Dean Mahomed (1759–1851) began his travel
memoir by professing to satisfy the curiosity of his
European readers about his Indian background:
'I find you have been very anxious to be made
acquainted with the early part of my Life, and the
History of my Travels: I shall be happy to gratify you.'[1]
The first Indian to publish in English, Mahomed
stands apart from his fellow countrymen who had also
travelled to England and Ireland in the eighteenth
century. A trickle of Indian sailors, servants, Anglo-
Indian children and their mothers, the occasional
scholar, and an Indian dignitary or two may have
entered Ireland and England at the same time, but
nobody had embarked on the kind of multi-faceted
career that distinguished Mahomed's trajectory:
initially as an author in Cork, later as a restaurateur
in London who sold the first plates of curry to English
customers, and finally as 'shampooing surgeon' or
masseur to George IV and William IV in Brighton.[2]

Born in Patna, India, in May 1759, Dean Mahomed
was the younger son of an Indian officer in the East
India Company's Army stationed in Bengal. After his
father's untimely death, he became a camp follower
when he was only eleven years old and was assigned
to Ensign Godfrey Evan Baker of the Bengal Army's

Sake Dean Mahomed
Shampooing Surgeon. Brighton
Thomas Mann Baynes, 1820s
Hand-coloured lithograph
on paper
262 x 223 mm (10 ³/₈ x 8 ³/₄")
Wellcome Library

Third European Regiment. In 1781 Mahomed was appointed *jemadar* (Indian ensign) of the elite grenadier company of the Second Battalion, Thirtieth Sepoy Regiment, Second Brigade. He fought at Kalpi against the Marathas in 1781 and in the same year helped rescue Warren Hastings when the Governor-General was trapped in a conflict with Raja Chayt Singh of Benares. Promoted to the rank of *subedar* (Indian lieutenant) for his service, Mahomed assisted in subduing peasant rebellions against British rule in the wake of Chayt Singh's defeat, near Ghazipur and Jaunpur.[3]

In July 1782, Hastings recalled Baker from active duty in disgrace following accusations that he had extorted money from villagers in the Benares region. Three months later Baker resigned from the Army and returned to his homeland, Ireland. Mahomed followed suit and accompanied him to Cork in 1784.[4]

A 24-year-old Mahomed arrived in Ireland, swiftly gaining entry into elite Anglo-Irish Protestant circles thanks to his close association with Baker, who belonged to a prominent landowning family. Baker also arranged for him to study English, a language that allowed Mahomed to communicate fluently with the citizens of his adopted country, as well as to write his travel memoir. But before publishing his book, in 1786 Mahomed eloped with a young teenager, an Anglo-Irish gentlewoman named Jane Daly. By this time it is likely that he had converted to Christianity and had become a member of the Protestant Church. The couple were married in an Anglican wedding ceremony in the diocese of Cork and Ross.[5]

While his marriage may have validated his social standing further, it was Mahomed's writing that probably established him as a well-bred man. In 1793 he proposed to publish his travel memoir by subscription in a series of newspaper advertisements. Entitled *The Travels of Dean Mahomet, a Native of Patna in Bengal, Through Several Parts of India While in the Service of The Honourable The East India Company. Written by Himself, In a Series of Letters to a Friend*, it immediately garnered support from an impressive number of 320 subscribers, a successful launch for a new literary figure in Cork society.[6] Published in the form of letters, Mahomed's recollections followed the eighteenth-century norm of describing travel experiences in an epistolary style.

If his travel memoir helped mediate his social rank as a foreigner within the higher echelons of polite Anglo-Irish society, Mahomed's reputation as an anglicised gentleman was only confirmed visually in his portrait engraved by J. Finley. Entitled *Dean Mahomet, an East Indian*, it is displayed as the frontispiece image of the book and depicts Mahomed as a fashionable, well-coiffed young man wearing an elaborate cravat. Set within an oval frame, the engraved half-length portrait was a familiar device used by artists to display the heads of famous individuals, most notably demonstrated in James Granger's compendious 1769 catalogue, *A Biographical History of England … consisting of Characters disposed in different Classes, and adapted to a methodical Catalogue of Engraved British Heads intended as an Essay towards reducing our Biography to System, and a Help to the*

The Travels of Dean Mahomet, a Native of Patna in Bengal, Through Several Parts of India While in the Service of The Honourable The East India Company. Written by Himself, In a Series of Letters to a Friend
Sake Dean Mahomed, 1794
Printed book
Page 175 x 120 mm (6⁷/₈ x 4³/₄")
The British Library

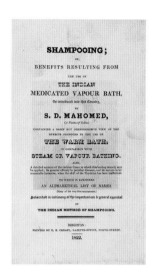

Shampooing; or, benefits
resulting from the use of the
Indian medicated vapour bath
Sake Dean Mahomed, 1822
Printed book
Page 223 x 137 mm (8³/₄ x 5³/₈")
The British Library

*Knowledge of Portraits … and answer the various purposes
of Medals.* Painted or printed, the oval portrait evoked
the tradition of heads portrayed on ancient Greek
and Roman coins and medals.[7] Believed to be
accurate representations of famous figures, such
images also commemorated grand deeds and events
associated with those they depicted.[8]

Within such a framework, Dean Mahomed's
portrait in his book not only allowed his readers
to put a face to his personal narrative, but also
presented him within the established artistic practice
of depicting noteworthy personalities. Thus he is
shown aligned more closely with the culture of his
adopted homeland than with that which he had left
behind. As such, he is also distinguished from his
fellow Indian immigrants. Yet discernible signs of
his cultural background are not entirely erased,
for the portrait categorises him as 'an East Indian',
articulating his origins. Furthermore, in his text
Mahomed traces his family roots to the Nawabs of
Murshidabad in the eighteenth-century Mughal
capital of Bengal.[9] At the same time, his dress and
hairstyle render him a hybrid character, visibly
different in race and colour from his audience but
well versed in their customs.

Mahomed continued to be shown dressed as a
respectable gentleman in another engraved portrait
by W. Maddocks exhibited on the title page of his
treatise on shampooing, first published in 1822, and
in a lithograph printed by Thomas Mann Baynes
(early nineteenth-century; see p. 78) and a portrait
painted by Samuel Drummond (1820).[10] While the

external elements of dress and deportment demonstrate the extent of his cultural assimilation, they simultaneously emphasise his dark skin and distinctly Indian appearance. His fluency in English, however, together with his familiarity with the rhetoric and structure of the travel narrative, cut across racial and social boundaries. The young writer borrowed heavily from other travel memoirs, such as Jemima Kindersley's *Letters from the Island of Teneriffe, Brazil, the Cape of Good Hope, and the East Indies* (London, 1777) and John Henry Grose's *A Voyage to the East Indies with Observations* (London, 1757, 1766, 1772).[11] And by penning his recollections of a distant land, he positioned himself among the many English diarists who had also written about their own foreign travel experiences.[12]

Sake Dean Mahomed
Samuel Drummond, 1820
Oil on canvas
670 x 540 mm (26 3/8 x 21 1/4")
Royal Pavilion, Libraries and Museums, Brighton & Hove

An anglicised Indian, Mahomed was in some respects a counterpart to the 'nabob', an Englishman who had built his fortune in India, and in certain cases even adopted Indian customs. A controversial figure, the nabob was frequently satirised on account of his wealth and sunburned skin. Mahomed seems to have resisted parallel attacks by presenting himself as an educated man of letters. Yet, like the nabob who intrigued his British onlookers, an anglicised Mahomed also caught the attention of fellow Indians he encountered such as Abu Talib, a Muslim diplomat who visited Cork in 1799 and wrote about their meeting many years later.[13]

Around 1807, Mahomed and his family relocated to London where he began working for a wealthy Scottish nabob, the Hon. Basil Cochrane, who had just returned from India and settled in a mansion in Portman Square. Cochrane opened a vapour bath in his home and Mahomed drew upon his skills in shampooing or therapeutic massage that he had learned in India. But by 1809 he struck out on his own when he opened the Hindostanee Coffee House near Portman Square, where he served Indian food and offered hookahs.[14] Now a restaurateur who relied on his Indian roots to market his new business, Mahomed's identity was a far cry from that of the anglicised author of a travel memoir. Unfortunately the establishment proved too expensive to maintain, and the entrepreneur found himself bankrupt after just a few years.[15] By 1814, he had embarked on the final phase of his career, as a bathhouse keeper in the fashionable seaside resort of Brighton.

SAKE DEEN MAHOMED,

Born May 8th. 1749, at Patna Hindoostan.

Died February 24th. 1851, at Brighton

In the 102nd Year of his age

Mahomed's entry into the flourishing town coincided with the building of the Brighton Pavilion, John Nash's orientalist architectural fantasy designed for George IV, in which Indian features were fused with chinoiserie in a tumbling trail of whimsical patterns and forms. As he had done in his restaurant in London, Mahomed capitalised on Indian products, from toothpowder to hair dye, Indian medicated vapour baths to shampooing oils. Unlike the Hindostanee Coffee House, however, the vapour bath business flourished to the extent that by 1818 he began promoting himself as a 'shampooing surgeon', and advertised his skills in his 1820 book, *Cases Cured by Sake Deen Mahomed, Shampooing Surgeon, and Inventor of the Indian Medicated Vapour and Sea-Water Baths, Written by the Patients Themselves.* His

Sake Dean Mahomed
Jean Pierre Feulard, c.1819
Watercolour and bodycolour
on ivory with gum arabic
110 x 85 mm (4³/₈ x 3³/₈")
Royal Pavilion, Libraries and
Museums, Brighton & Hove

**Waistcoat and shoes worn by
Sake Dean Mahomed**
c.1810–30
Velvet, silk, leather and metal
Royal Pavilion, Libraries and
Museums, Brighton & Hove

professional success culminated in the building
of 'Mahomed's Baths' near the Pavilion, where he
catered to fashionable male and female clients.

Mahomed's reputation would be sealed when
he was appointed royal 'shampooing surgeon' to
Their Majesties Kings George IV and William IV. In
addition, he supplied the royal household with bath
products and even inserted the royal coat of arms
into his newspaper advertisements. By 1822 he had
dedicated his treatise on shampooing to George IV,
one of his many public claims of loyalty to the royal
family. Published in three editions in 1822, 1826, and
1838, the book expanded on the medical benefits of
shampooing and was bolstered by Mahomed's self-
proclaimed native expertise.[16]

Royal connections necessitated an official
court dress. Depicted in a hand-coloured lithograph
by Thomas Mann Baynes (p. 78), the actual outfit still
survives in the collection of the Brighton Museum
and Art Gallery. In addition to a variation of the
traditional Indian silk *kurta* (tunic) and *pyjamas*
(trousers), Mahomed incorporated other details such
as a cummerbund, dagger and turban, together with
European accessories such as a waistcoat, necktie
and yellow gloves. He stands in front of a building
reminiscent of the Brighton Pavilion, whose fusion
of Indian and European styles echoes the hybrid
nature of his own appearance. In this regard, Baynes's
portrait does justice to the porous boundaries of
cultural identity that his sitter characterised.
Anglicised yet Indian, his figure evokes an aura of
aristocracy through his elaborate attire as well as his

links with the royal family conveyed by the Pavilion. Be it the 'shampooing surgeon' or the King's ornate seaside palace, each entity is shaped by the cross-fertilisation of different aesthetic frameworks, which in turn reflects cultural overlaps and intersections. Reinvented as an exotic curiosity, Mahomed's image resonates with an Indian eccentricity, on which local observers in Brighton also commented in their newspaper reports.[17] At the same time, it parallels his repeated emphasis on his unique background and knowledge in order to distinguish himself from his rivals and promote his business.[18]

Dean Mahomed died in Brighton on 24 February 1851, the same year that the Great Exhibition opened in London to celebrate British imperial progress in technology and commerce.

NOTES

1 Dean Mahomet, *The Travels of Dean Mahomet, a Native of Patna in Bengal, Through Several Parts of India While in the Service of The Honourable The East India Company. Written by Himself, In a Series of Letters to A Friend. In Two Volumes*, Cork, 1794, vol. 1, p. B.

2 Fisher 1997, p. 135; Visram 1986, pp. 10–20; Fisher 2004, pp. 71–102.

3 M.H. Fisher, 'Mahomed, Deen (1759–1851), Shampooing Surgeon and Restaurateur', *Oxford Dictionary of National Biography*, Oxford, 2004 (accessed 23 September 2004: www.oxforddnb.com/view/article/53351); Fisher 1997,

pp. 24–30.

4 Fisher 2004.

5 Op. cit.; Fisher 1997, pp. 135–7; Fisher 1996, pp. 202–9.

6 Fisher 1997, pp. 214–18.

7 Pointon 1993, pp. 65–6. Pointon also demonstrates that such imagery relied on the ancient paradigm of the *imago clipeata*, a concept associated with circular shields carried by soldiers at war that bore the emperor's images. Such representations were devoid of any hint of a particular setting or context. Similarly, eighteenth-century engraved heads isolated

the sitter's likeness, focusing attention on the subject's identity.

8 Haskell 1995, p. 27; see also pp. 1–26, 36–79.

9 Fisher 1996, p. 16.

10 The engraved portrait can be seen in Sake Dean Mahomed, *Shampooing, or, Benefits Resulting from the Use of the Indian Medicated Vapour Bath: as Introduced into this Country by S. D. Mahomed ... Containing a Brief but Comprehensive View of the effects Produced by the Use of the Warm Bath, in Comparison with Steam or Vapour Bathing*, Brighton, 1822, 1826, 1838.

11 Fisher 1996, p. 227.

12 For more about the scope and significance of travel narratives, see Stoye 1989, p. 3.

13 Fisher 1997, pp. 142–4.

14 Op. cit. pp. 150–2.

15 Fisher 1996, pp. 257–66; Fisher 1997, pp. 149–53.

16 Fisher 1996, pp. 267–82; Fisher 1997, pp. 153–78; Gilbert 1949, pp. 35–6.

17 Fisher 1997, p. 175.

18 Op. cit. p. 171.

SARTJEE, THE HOTTENTOT VENUS,

EXHIBITING AT Nº 225, PICCADILLY.

7 Sara Baartman

David Bindman

The story of Sara or Saartjie Baartman, a Khoikhoi woman brought from South Africa and exhibited in a public show in Piccadilly in 1810, is a distressing one to twenty-first-century observers, as it was to many at the time. She was treated as a 'living curiosity', like an exotic animal, to be compared with 'the Irish Giant' and George Lambert who was enormously fat, on account of her (by European standards) exceptionally large buttocks. In Paris, where she went in 1814, she was also part of a popular show but she attracted the attention of the comparative anatomist Georges Cuvier and his colleagues,[1] and when she died there at the end of the same year her body was dissected and the results published. Her remains were preserved in what was to become the Musée de l'Homme in Paris, and body parts with a cast of her body and her skeleton were on display until the 1970s. They were returned to South Africa for burial in 2002 after a personal request to the French Government from Nelson Mandela.

The so-called 'Hottentot Venus' was exhibited in London dressed in a transparent garment so that 'the enormous size of her posterior parts are visible as if the said female were naked',[2] but her display attracted

Poster announcing the appearance of Sara Baartman
1811
Letterpress
490 x 290 mm (19 3/8 x 11 3/8 ")
The British Library

Saartjee, The Hottentot Venus. Exhibiting at No. 225 Piccadilly
? Lewis, published by S. Baartman, 14 March 1811
Etching and aquatint
420 x 290 mm (16 5/8 x 11 3/8 ")
The British Library

Saartjee, The Hottentot Venus
Published by Hendrick Cezar,
18 September 1810
Etching and aquatint
559 x 406 mm (22 x 16")
The British Museum

SARTJEE THE HOTENTOT VENUS
from Gamoos River South Africa

**Sartjee. The Hottentot Venus
from Gamoos River South Africa**
Unknown artist, c.1811
Coloured etching
395 x 265 mm (15½ x 10⅜")
The British Museum

disgust at the time, for it was believed by anti-slavery campaigners, who had seen the slave trade abolished in England in 1807, that she was a victim of what a correspondent to a newspaper, calling himself 'An Englishman', described as 'that most horrid of all situations, *slavery*'.[3] The African Association brought a court case with the intention of freeing Baartman on the grounds that she was 'exhibited for money, against her consent'. A contract with Alexander Dunlop, an English exporter of exotic animals from the Cape, who had brought her over in partnership

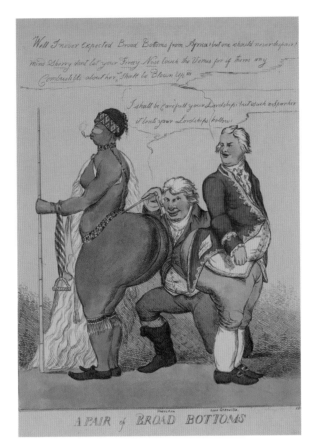

Well I never expected Broad Bottoms from Africa; but one should never despair!
mind Sherry don't let your Firey Nose touch the Venus for if there's any
Combustible about her, "shall be Blown up,"

I shall be carefull your Lordship; but such a Sparkler
it beats your Lordships (hollow)

Sheredan   Lord Grenville.

A PAIR of BROAD BOTTOMS

A Pair of Broad Bottoms
Unknown artist, 1810
Coloured etching
375 x 270 mm (14 3/4 x 10 5/8 ")
The British Museum

with the South African Hendrick Cezar, was produced in court, stating that Dunlop would take care of medical expenses and pay her an annual wage of twelve guineas for five years. On being cross-examined in Dutch, she asserted her consent to being put on display. She spoke up for herself in court without protest at her situation, giving signs of a strong personality who did not willingly accept the role of victim.

Her appearance on show in London is accurately recorded in a fine aquatint (reproduced on p. 88)

The Court at Brighton
a la Chinese!!
George Cruikshank, 1825
Coloured etching
406 x 559 mm (16 x 22")
The British Museum

signed by 'Lewis' and published by Baartman herself
at the address in Piccadilly where she was displayed,
no doubt intending it to be sold at the event. An
image also exists in a version published by Cezar.[4]

This etching and aquatint was much copied,
and it encouraged a number of coarse and ribald
caricatures that traded on the fact that the political
opposition under Lord Grenville were known as the
'Broad Bottoms'. This is the context for the joke, to
give one example, of the anonymous caricature *A Pair
of Broad Bottoms* of 1810 (see p. 91), where Grenville's

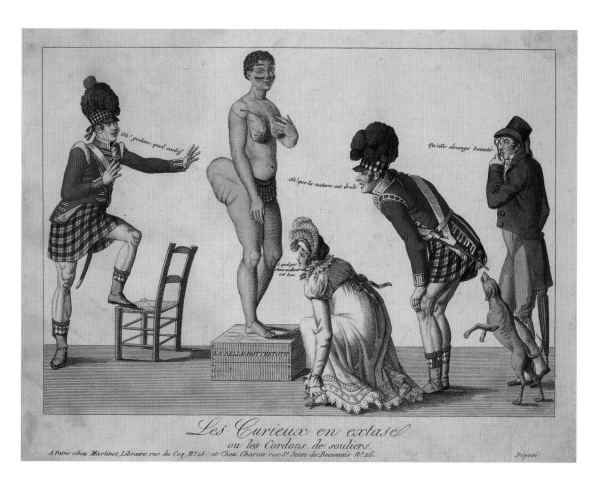

Les Curieux en extase
ou les Cordons de souliers.
A Paris chez Martinet, Libraire, rue du Coq, N.º 15 et Chez Charon rue St Jean de Beauvais N.º 26. Déposé

buttocks are shown as almost a match for Sara
Baartman's. The joke had some longevity, for a statue
of Baartman in profile is compared with a profile of
the Prince of Wales in the background of a print of
1825 by George Cruikshank satirising life in the
Brighton Pavilion, entitled *The Court at Brighton a la
Chinese!!*.

　　After the exhibition in London Baartman seems
to have embarked on a provincial tour, which
included Manchester, where she was baptised, before
arriving in Paris in 1814. Her appearance there caused

**Les Curieux en extase ou
les cordons de souliers**
Unknown artist, 1815
Coloured etching
235 x 310 mm (9¼ x 12¼")
The British Museum

Femme de race Bochismann
After de Wailly, Geoffrey-Saint-
Hilaire and Frédéric Cuvier, 1824
Coloured lithograph
490 x 290 mm (19⅜ x 11⅜")
The British Library

a sensation comparable to that in London, and it was similarly the subject of such coarse caricatures as *Les Curieux en extase*, which shows her being gawped at by, among others, two kilted Scotsmen. In Paris, however, she attracted another and more serious constituency from the scientific community, who saw her as a fascinating link in the history of mankind. Georges Cuvier, the famous comparative anatomist and pioneer of 'racial science', and his colleagues from the Musée d'Histoire Naturelle were able to examine her alive and dissect her body after her death on 29 December 1815, producing some fine watercolour paintings of her. Though Cuvier recognised Baartman's command of languages and personality, his view of her was conditioned by the then-current theory of the gradation of humanity,[5] which saw a continuum from ape through African to the highest form of mankind, the European, with the 'Boschimanne' or Bushman race, to which Cuvier thought she belonged, at the lowest level of humanity. Thus Cuvier was caught between his belief that Baartman was close in physiognomy to an orang-utan, and his recognition of her as a spirited individual with a good memory and accomplished enough to pick up Dutch, English and French. Baartman consented to be painted frontally and from the side in watercolour, and the paintings, which are poignant in their suggestion of a person treated like a scientific specimen, are now in the collection of the Muséum national d'Histoire naturelle in Paris.

Baartman was also an object of scientific curiosity for another reason. It had long been noted that

Khoikhoi women had what was known as a tablier, a flap of skin hanging down from the genital area. This was firmly established by Cuvier to be an extension of part of the vulva and not fundamentally different from other women. Nonetheless, it increased the air of sexuality that surrounded her and led to her genitals being preserved and exhibited after her death.

We have, then, a contrast between Baartman's treatment in London and Paris. In London she was a 'show', a human curiosity, in which her physical attributes were the subject of ribaldry, and she was treated like an animal in the zoo, despite the disgust that many felt at this inhumane treatment. In Paris she was similarly an object of popular spectacle, but she also attracted scientific curiosity, both in life and death, as a representative of the most 'primitive' type of African. It is useless to argue which was the worse treatment; they were both unacceptably demeaning to a woman who showed herself to be far from passive in the cruelly humiliating situation in which she found herself.

NOTES

1 Honour 1989, pp. 52–4.

2 From the Court Records, see Qureshi 2004, p. 236.

3 Op. cit. p. 238.

4 The only impression I have found of the print published by Baartman herself is in album 1.2 of Lysons' *Collectanea* in the British Library, which also contains invaluable press cuttings and other material. The version published by Cezar is in the British Museum.

5 Stepan 1982, pp. 13–14.

8 Raja Rammohun Roy

Romita Ray

Raja Rammohun Roy (1772/4–1833) is best known as
the Hindu reformer who founded the *Brahmo Sabha*
(later *Samaj*) or Theistic Society of God in 1828.
Probably born in 1772 (although the birthdate
inscribed on his tombstone is 1774) in Radhanagar,
Burdwan district, Bengal, about a hundred miles
from Calcutta, Rammohun was the youngest child
of Ramkanta Roy (d.1803), a *zemindar* or landowner,
and his second wife Tarini Devi. While his family's
hereditary title was Bandyopadhyay or Banerji, the
princely title of Roy had been given by the Nawab
of Bengal to Krishna Chandra Banerji, Rammohun's
great-grandfather, who passed it on to his
descendants.[1]

As was customary among Rarhi Brahmans,
Rammohun Roy was married three times when he
was still a child, a tradition he later criticised and
censured. Accurate information about this early phase
of his life, however, is sparse and often uncertain.
For instance, very little is known about his marriages
except that his first wife died very young but his
last wife survived him. His second wife, who died in
1824, bore him two sons: Radhaprasad (b.1800) and
Ramaprasad (b.1812), born a few years before their
father moved to Calcutta. He also had an adopted

'Ram Mohan Roy'
Unknown artist, *c.*1820
Gouache on ivory
125 x 100 mm (5 x 4")
Victoria and Albert Museum

son, Rajaram, who travelled with him to England.

A talented linguist from childhood, the young Rammohun was probably sent to study Persian and Arabic in Patna, where he apparently read the Koran alongside Arabic translations of Aristotle and Euclid's writings. His father subsequently sent him to learn Sanksrit in Benares, where he became well versed in Hindu literature, law and philosophy. But Persian was still the official courtly language preferred by Indian rulers, a legacy of the Mughal era and retained by the East India Company.[2] So proficient was Rammohun in the Indo-Islamic languages that he wrote his earliest extant writing, the treatise *Tuhfat-al-muwahhiddin* (*A Gift to Monotheists*), published in Murshidabad in 1803–4, in Persian with an Arabic introduction. In this tract he emphasised the notion that all religions were united in their belief in One Universal Supreme Being.

Following his father's death in 1803, Rammohun began working as *diwan* or financial officer for John Digby, the tax collector at Rangpur. At the time Rammohun's knowledge of English was still rudimentary but his interactions with Digby improved his command of the language. He soon became so fluent in reading, writing and speaking English that from 1816 onwards he began publishing regularly in the language with which he had once struggled. An astute businessman on the side, after a decade of working for the British Government, trading with the East India Company, loaning them money and investing in more land, he retired a wealthy man when he was only forty-two years old.

Rammohun settled in Calcutta, where he spent the rest of his life devoted to writing and to social and religious reform. In 1815 he founded the *Atmiya Sabha* (Society of Friends), whose members met regularly to discuss social and religious subjects, and theological issues.[3] Within a short period of time he had gathered together a small but influential group of Indian and European friends, including Dwarkanath Tagore and Prasanna Kumar Tagore, wealthy landowners, successful merchants and prominent members of the city's Bengali elite, as well as David Hare, whom he helped establish the Hare School in 1818.[4]

The first Indian intellectual to write in a modern European language, Rammohun made public his ideas and opinions about Hinduism, the caste system, ritual and idolatry through his books. Although other Indians such as Sake Dean Mahomed, Joseph Emin and Meer Hassan Ali also published works in English in the late eighteenth and early nineteenth centuries, their contributions did not tackle Hindu social and religious issues: Mahomed and Emin penned their travel memoirs, while Hassan Ali wrote about the grammar of the 'Hindoostanie Language'.[5]

By 1815, Rammohun had begun publishing his translations of Vedantic literature,[6] beginning with a Bengali translation of the *Vedanta-Sutras* that was accompanied by a summary of the same work in English, Bengali and Hindustani. These were followed by his translations of the *Kena Upanisad* and *Isopanisad* in 1816, and of the *Katha, Mundaka* and *Mundukyu Upanisads* in 1817. In his prefaces to these

Translation of an Abridgment of the Vedant, or Resolution of all the Veds; the Most Celebrated and Revered Work of Brahminical Theology; Establishing the Unity of the Supreme Being; and that He Alone is the Object of Propitiation and Worship
Rammohun Roy, 1817
Printed document
Page 236 x 179 mm (9¼ x 7")
The British Library

Rammohun's critiques of Hinduism may have generated heated discussion, but they also brought valuable attention to key issues and such highly problematic traditions as *sati*, the custom of widows burning themselves on the funeral pyres of their dead husbands. His interest in *sati* was influenced by the horrifying death of his sister-in-law, who followed the custom when his brother Jagamohun was cremated in 1811. A witness to the incident, Rammohun began campaigning against the tradition, first by frequenting cremation grounds in Calcutta where he tried dissuading women on the brink of sacrificing their lives, and later by writing about the inhumanity of such a custom.

volumes he continued to censure image-worship, priestly rights and privileges, and religious rituals. His ideas did not take long to catch the attention of orthodox Hindus such as Sankara Sastri in Madras and Mrityunjay Vidyalankar in Calcutta, who defended their stance and attacked his ideas through their own writings.[7] Such debate only strengthened Rammohun's growing reputation as an intellectual and reformer who did not shy away from criticising such time-honoured Hindu customs as the worship of deities, the emphasis on elaborate ceremonies and the rigid devotion to the caste system, among others.

If the pen is mightier than the sword, then his publications condemning *sati* certainly stirred more discussion and clarified the need for action.[8] His first tract on the subject was published in Bengali in 1818 and was followed by an English translation in November of that same year. Entitled *A Conference between an Advocate for, and an Opponent of the Practice of Burning Widows Alive*, it paved the way for yet another tract nearly three times the length of the first, published in February 1820. Dedicated to the Marchioness of Hastings, he clearly targeted readers powerful enough to initiate the necessary social changes. The English press responded favourably to his agitations, hailing him as a reformer. Divisions were deeper in the vernacular press in India, however, with newspapers such as the *Samachar Darpan* and the *Sambad Kaumudi* supporting Rammohun's stance and clashing, as a result, with the pro-*sati* stance of the *Samachar Chandrika*. But Rammohun was not the only individual to rally against *sati*: others, like William

Carey, the Serampore missionary, and M.H. Brooke,
a collector at Shahabad, also condemned the custom
and took action in their own ways. But the highly
controversial subject continued to evade the
attention of successive Governor-Generals until 1829,
when *sati* was finally abolished by the then Governor-
General, Lord William Bentinck, a protégé of Jeremy
Bentham.[9]

Rammohun's criticism of Hinduism also appealed
to the Baptist missionaries stationed in Serampore,
who engaged him to translate the Gospels into
Bengali. He began studying Hebrew and Greek in
order to read the Bible in different languages, and
in 1820 he published his reflections on biblical
literature in *The Precepts of Jesus: The Guide to Peace
and Happiness; extracted from the Books of the New
Testament, ascribed to the Four Evangelists. With
Translations in Sanskrit and Bengali.* Ever the critical
voice, he compared the Holy Trinity to Hindu idolatry,
angering the Serampore missionaries who challenged
his ideas in their journal *The Friend of India.* The
debate continued and Rammohun responded with
other tracts defending his thoughts about the
Gospels, advocating instead a Unitarian
interpretation.[10]

A belief in the oneness of God rather than in
the traditional Christian faith in the Holy Trinity
(Father, Son and Holy Spirit) distinguished
Unitarianism, whose organised church emerged from
the Protestant Reformation of the sixteenth century.
In 1823, Rammohun Roy helped William Adam
establish the Unitarian mission in Calcutta. Later, in

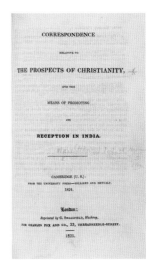

Correspondence Relative to
the Prospects of Christianity,
and the Means of Promoting
its Reception in India
William Adam and
Rammohun Roy, 1825
Printed book
Page 140 x 128 mm (5 ¹/₂ x 5 ")
The British Library

London, he mingled with such eminent Unitarians as Jeremy Bentham, William Godwin, Robert Owen and Lucy Aikin. He also corresponded with American Unitarians like Henry Ware, the distinguished Harvard professor, and Jared Sparks, the first Unitarian minister in Baltimore.

Rammohun's liberal ideas, together with his Unitarian sentiments, led to the foundation of the *Brahmo Samaj* in 1828. Devoted to a monotheistic form of worship, its followers dismissed idolatry and turned instead to the *Vedas*, the ancient Hindu scriptures. Open to members of all castes, as well as to Christians, Jews and Muslims, the ministry of the *Brahmo Samaj* still relied on Brahmins in accordance with Brahminical practice. At its core, however, it upheld the reforms in Hinduism in favour of which Rammohun had advocated for so many years.[11] Its success revealed Rammohun's heroic determination to modernise one of the most resilient entities of nineteenth-century India – Hinduism, enmeshed in its complicated web of deep-rooted beliefs, customs, and rituals elaborated and incorporated over the centuries.

By 1823 he made yet another move to modernise the country by supporting the English system of education for Indians rather than the traditional Sanskrit one. Although he had devoted much of his own scholarly career to studying Sanskrit literature, he believed that the English system had potential to create progress and reform by uprooting superstition and idol-worship.[12]

In November 1830, Rammohun Roy journeyed to

England on behalf of Akbar II, the titular Mughal Emperor of Delhi, to negotiate an increase in the Emperor's pension. By then Akbar had also conferred the title 'Raja' upon him.[13] The first Indian intellectual to sail across the seas to Europe, otherwise strictly forbidden by Hindu tradition at the time, Rammohun was, however, thwarted by the British Government who refused to recognise him as the Emperor's official envoy.[14] Despite this initial obstacle, he embarked on his journey accompanied by his adopted son Rajaram, his trusted associate, and servants. Received enthusiastically in England, he delivered sermons and speeches and continued to publish. Unitarians especially welcomed him, believing that his liberal views overlapped with theirs. He met James Mill and Jeremy Bentham, whose ideas he had long admired, attended the coronation of King William IV in Westminster Abbey, visited Paris, and planned trips to Austria and Italy.

During his stay in London Rammohun Roy rented a house in Cumberland Terrace and hired a carriage with a liveried coachman and footman.[15] He continued, however, to be dressed in traditional clothing. An anonymous account, written on 19 March 1832, records his striking appearance: 'His dress was magnificent – a purple [?] robe, bordered with rich gold lace – a vest of crimson, embroidered with gold & variegated shawl crossed round the waist, & tied behind, with a [?] gold buckle fastening his robe in front.'[16] This description complements the full-length portrait of Rammohun painted by Henry Perronet Briggs that same year (Bristol City Museum and Art

Letter from Rammohun Roy to an unidentified correspondent
1 June 1833
Ink on paper
188 x 116 mm (7 3/8 x 4 5/8 ")
The British Library

Rammohun Roy makes arrangements to accompany an unknown lady to chapel. His letter mentions noted figures Rev. Willliam Johnson Fox and Edward Tagart.

Raja Ram Mohun Roy
Unknown artist, 1833
Watercolour on paper
128 x 105 mm (5 x 4⅛")
The British Library

Gallery; fig. 6, p. 17), in which he is portrayed as a
scholar holding a book and strolling through an
imaginary rendering of the Bengal landscape.

In 1833, the famous American artist Rembrandt
Peale also painted a portrait of Rammohun (Peabody
Essex Museum; fig. 5, p. 16), a picture he later sold to
the Boston Athenaeum. The two met because Peale
had been asked to deliver a letter to the Hindu
reformer by his close friend, the Unitarian minister
Jared Sparks.[17] Distinguished by his moustache, black
hair and turban, Rammohun was probably easily
identified by his imposing appearance. A portrait
painted in profile by an unknown artist in 1833
depicts him dressed as a member of the Bengali
gentry with a shawl thrown over his shoulder and a

turban on his head. A very similar image had been reproduced in 1823 as the frontispiece to *The Precepts of Jesus*, thereby circulating his image in Britain and America.

As well as mingling with philosophers, artists and writers in London, Rammohun pursued the original goal of his visit, to represent Akbar II. He submitted the Mughal Emperor's case to the Court of Directors in his pamphlet *Treaty with the King of Delhi* (1831), and managed to obtain a minimal increase in the Emperor's pension. He also appealed to the Privy Council to retain the 1829 legislation against *sati*.

Although widely recognised for his intellectual contributions and social activism, Rammohun spent the last years of his life battling financial difficulty and poor health. He died on a trip to Bristol on 27 September 1833. His death was mourned by his supporters and in the British press.[18]

NOTES

1 Salmond 2004, p. 43; D. Killingley, 'Roy, Rammohun (1772? –1833)', *Oxford Dictionary of National Biography*, Oxford, 2004 www.oxforddnb.com/view/article/47673, accessed 22 April 2006.

2 On the importance of Sanskrit and Persian during the British Raj, see Cohn 1996, pp. 22–30.

3 Salmond 2004, pp. 44–7.

4 Cromwell Crawford 1987, pp. 46–7. Nearly a decade after his close friend Rammohun Roy died in Bristol, the brilliant entrepreneur, *zemindar* and civic leader Dwarkanath Tagore also sailed to London, in 1842, returning to Calcutta after almost eleven months of travelling. Three years later he visited London again, where he died on 1 August 1845. See Kling 1976, pp. 168–75, 230–7.

5 Fisher 2004, pp. 81, 127.

6 Vedantic literature is the corpus of writing devoted to the study and analysis of the *Vedas*, the ancient Hindu scriptures.

7 Salmond 2004, pp. 47–8.

8 Cromwell Crawford 1987, p. 105.

9 Salmond 2004, p. 46; Cromwell Crawford 1987, pp. 102–9.

10 Salmond 2004, p. 47; Zastoupil 2002, pp. 215–29.

11 Cromwell Crawford 1987, pp. 86–92. The *Brahmo Samaj* was rivalled by another group called the *Dharma Sabha*, formed by orthodox Hindus and led by Raja Radhakanta Deb.

12 Salmond 2004, p. 47.

13 Although the term 'Raja' usually means king or princely ruler, in the case of Rammohun Roy it was awarded as a social rank in accordance with Mughal imperial protocol.

14 Fisher 2004, p. 251; Salmond 2004, p. 47.

15 Fisher 2004, pp. 252–4.

16 India Office Collection, British Library, MSS Eur B259.

17 Langlais Dodge and Bean 2000, pp. 71–4.

18 Fisher 2004, pp. 257–9.

9 Maharaja Dalip Singh

Romita Ray

On 10 July 1854, Queen Victoria noted in her journal that Franz Winterhalter 'was in ecstasies at the beauty and nobility of the young Maharajah', referring to Dalip Singh (1838–93), Maharaja of Lahore, who had caught her attention when he gained a royal audience with her soon after arriving in London.[1] The last Sikh ruler of the Punjab, and the youngest son of Maharaja Ranjit Singh (1780–1839) and his junior queen, Rani Jindan Kaur (1817–63), Dalip Singh was born in Lahore on 6 September 1838.[2] A romantic figure in the eyes of the English Queen, the young exiled Maharaja's glittering entrance into London's elite social circles contrasted sharply with his frustrating inability to rule his kingdom and his financial troubles.

His idyllic childhood was punctuated by the grim violence of anarchy and war. On 21 September 1845 he witnessed the execution of his beloved maternal uncle, Prime Minister Jawahar Singh, by the powerful Khalsa Army, a memory that continued to haunt him for the rest of his life. Nearly a year later, on 11 March 1846, the same army surrendered to the British at the end of the first Anglo-Sikh War. The Sikh kingdom began crumbling as the British parcelled off Jammu and Kashmir to Gulab Singh, annexed the territory

Dalip Singh on the Lower Terrace at Osborne House, 23 August 1854
Dr Ernst Becker, 1889
Carbon print
160 x 200 mm (6¼ x 7⅞")
Lent by Her Majesty The Queen

After a series of bloody coups in the wake of Ranjit Singh's death in 1839, Dalip Singh came to the throne in 1843 when he was only five years old. Brought up with all the privileges of a Sikh prince, he enjoyed the sports of falconry, riding, shooting, hunting and wrestling, and was tutored in Persian and the Gurmukhi (Sikh) alphabet so that he could read the *Adi Granth*, the sacred scripture of Sikhism.

**Dalip Singh, the Durbar
of December 1845**
Hasan al-Din, 1845
Gouache with gold on
thick paper or board
145 x 182 mm (5 ⅝ x 7 ⅛")
The British Library

Bedecked in jewels, turban and courtly dress, the 7-year-old king is presented as a young warrior in keeping with the tenets of Guru Gobind Singh (1666–1708), who established the Khalsa or the brotherhood of Sikh men. The gun also invests the child with masculine power typically associated with grown men.

between the rivers Beas and Sutlej, and by the terms of the Treaty of Byrowal signed in December 1846, established a Council of Regency which, under the watchful eye of the British resident Henry Lawrence, ruled over the area that remained in the hands of the young Dalip Singh. Although the Council included Rani Jindan and was meant to govern the drastically reduced kingdom until the Maharaja came of age in 1854, its intervention in the Punjab signalled the finale of the powerful state that his father had created.

Two images of the boy king reveal some of his important transitions in India. Hasan al-Din's

rendering of Dalip Singh presiding over the Durbar
of December 1845 in the Anglo-Mughal style depicts
the monarch seated on a chair, holding a gun, with
a pet dog at his feet. No longer just a prince, he is
flanked by his financial minister Diwan Dina Nath
and minister of foreign affairs Fakir Nura al-Din to
his left, and by military commanders Tej Singh and
Labh Singh to his right; an attendant stands behind
him.[3]

Whereas Hasan al-Din's image of Dalip Singh
portrays him as a Sikh leader among members of his
court, George Beechey's picture of some seven years
later (private collection) presents him as a pensive
and solitary figure. Commissioned by the Governor-
General, Sir James Broun-Ramsay, Marquess of
Dalhousie, it shows Singh with a jewel-framed
miniature of Queen Victoria painted by Emily Eden
suspended from his pearl necklace.[4] A small yet
highly significant detail displayed prominently in
the portrait, such an image of the Queen in a picture
of the Sikh ruler establishes Dalip Singh as her
imperial subject. Painted twenty-four years before
Victoria was declared the Queen Empress of India
(1876), Beechey's composition nonetheless defines
the boy king's primary allegiance to the East India
Company and, by extension, to the British monarchy.
The miniature portrait of Victoria set in diamonds
had been gifted to Ranjit Singh in Lahore by William
Osborne on behalf of the Governor-General, Lord
Auckland (Emily Eden's brother) on 20 May 1838.[5]

If Beechey's portrait displays the young ruler as
a devoted follower of a monarch he was yet to meet,

then it also marks the painful separation between the
boy and his mother. In 1847 he had publicly refused
to follow British instructions to accept Tej Singh as
his commander-in-chief, a rebellious act believed to
have been instigated by Dalip's mother, Rani Jindan.
Dalip Singh was kidnapped and his mother placed
under house arrest, her pleas to have her son
returned to her ignored. A second Anglo-Sikh War
(1848–9) erupted, resulting in the Maharaja being
placed in the care of a Scottish army surgeon, John
Login. In November 1849 he was removed from the
Punjab to Fatehgarh, a remote town near Kanpur and
a centre of Christian missionary activity.

Dalip Singh would never return to his homeland.
In the summer of 1852 he was taken to Mussoori,
where he was immersed in the British colonial culture
of the hill-stations: playing cricket, shooting and
taking long walks in his picturesque surroundings.
His old associations were severed as he was gradually
anglicised.[6] Forbidden from corresponding with his
mother, Dalip Singh was not allowed to mingle with
other Sikhs, while his attendants were replaced by
Bhajan Lal, an employee of the British charged with
the responsibility of converting him to Christianity.[7]
In 1853 he became a Christian, his conversion praised
by Queen Victoria, who observed that he was 'the
first of his high rank' to have 'embraced our faith'.[8]
His cultural ties erased steadily, Dalip Singh's Sikh
background was anglicised further by his growing
command of English, gained at the expense of losing
his fluency over his mother tongue. By sacrificing his
religious roots and native language, he had emerged

Maharaja Dalip Singh
Franz Xaver Winterhalter, 1854
Oil on canvas
2038 x 1095 mm (80¼ x 43⅛")
The Royal Collection

instead as a hazy reminder of the heritage into which he had been born.

In May 1854 Dalip Singh arrived in London where he stayed at the fashionable Mivarts Hotel (later known as Claridges). Officially received by Queen Victoria at Buckingham Palace on 1 July, he impressed the British monarch with his manners to the extent that she took pity on his deposed status and promoted him to the rank of a European prince.[9] The Queen's favours continued, most notably exemplified by her commissioning his full-length portrait later the same year from Franz Xaver Winterhalter. Made to look much taller than he was in reality, the Maharaja appeared resplendent in his jewels, many of which had also been recorded earlier in the Beechey portrait, and which he was allowed to retain when the British authorities confiscated his land. These included the diamond aigrette and star pinned to his turban, his three strands of pearls, the additional pearl necklace with the painted miniature of Queen Victoria, his emerald and pearl earrings, and a ring also adorned with the Queen's portrait.[10] Transformed into an ornamental figure replete with the emblems of kingship, the portrait glosses over the absence of actual political power.

Painted between 10 and 17 July during two-hour sittings each day, Winterhalter's portrait presents the Sikh Maharaja with the vestiges of his inheritance. During one of his sittings a poignant moment occurred when the Queen arranged for the Koh-i-noor diamond to be brought from the Tower of London so that Dalip Singh could see it again.

In 1871 Dalip Singh reflected on his transformation in a sentimental letter to Lewin Bentham Bowring, once private secretary to Viscount Canning, Viceroy of India: 'I have not altogether forgotten Punjabee ... but of course not having an opportunity of speaking in that tongue habitually I could not hold a long conversation in it'.
Letter from Maharaja Dalip Singh to Lewin Bentham Bowring, 20 December 1871. Bowring Papers, British Library, MSS Eur G38/1 (Album 1).

Cut down and polished by a diamond cutter in Amsterdam, it was a powerful reminder of his absolute surrender to the East India Company at the cost of being severed from his family heritage and cultural past. According to Lady Login, after inspecting the diamond, Dalip Singh returned it with deference to the Queen as a 'loyal subject' would have given a valuable item to his 'Sovereign'.[11] It is as though the Koh-i-noor had been surrendered one more time, but now in the manner of bestowing a gift. Receiving news of this exchange, Lord Dalhousie allegedly called the gesture 'arrant humbug'.[12] A deeply charged transaction, it reiterated the sacrifice of Dalip Singh's family jewels, the ultimate homage paid by a colonial subject to the British monarch. The jewels that he still owned, and which adorn his figure in the portrait, were now the only tangible links to his past as the last Sikh ruler. As a Christian convert, save for the sword he no longer bore the other traditional emblems expected of Sikh males: the unshorn hair (kes), the comb (kangha), breeches (kacha) and the steel bracelet on his right wrist (kara).[13]

Dalip Singh continued to grow close to the Royal Family, and their friendship deepened despite the news of the horrific events of the Indian Rebellion of 1857. A frequent guest at Osborne House on the Isle of Wight, he also attended the marriage of the Princess Royal to Prince Frederick William of Prussia in 1858, and that of Albert Edward, the Prince of Wales to Princess Alexandra of Denmark in 1863.[14] With estates in Scotland and Yorkshire, and trips to Europe, Dalip Singh appeared to live the life of a

Letter from Maharaja Dalip Singh to an unnamed duke
24 June 1858
Ink on paper
180 x 112 mm (7 1/8 x 4 3/8 ")
The British Library

Dalip Singh accepts an invitation to a ball in London. The letter was written at Claridges, where the Maharaja had resided since his arrival in London four years earlier.

The Marriage of the Princess Royal to Prince Frederick William of Prussia, 25 January 1858
Egron Sellif Lundgren, 1858
Watercolour on paper
280 x 388 mm (11 x 15¼")
The Royal Collection

Dalip Singh can be seen among the guests seated in the front row of the balcony.

British aristocrat.[15] When he was in London, he also enjoyed the amusements of the fashionable and wealthy, attending soirées, balls, and other parties.

In 1859 he sailed to India to rescue his ailing mother from exile in Nepal. News of his reunion with her in Calcutta in 1861 spread swiftly, and he was besieged by former members of his court and by Sikh soldiers. An alarmed Lord Canning requested that he return to England with his mother. Rani Jindan sailed back to London with her son, only to die two years later. Dalip Singh returned once again to India to cremate her body. On his way back to England, he married Bamba Müller in Cairo on 7 June 1864. Part-Ethiopian and part-German, she had caught his eye at the American Presbyterian School when he had visited en route to India for his mother's funeral.[16] The couple set up residence at their newly acquired estate at Elveden in Suffolk, where, between 1866 and 1879, they had six children who were brought up amidst its sprawling splendour.[17]

In 1872, Ronald Melville persuaded the Maharaja to pursue a political career. Elected to the Carlton Club, he was supposed to stand against Gladstone's son for the Tory seat at Whitby. With Gladstone and Queen Victoria's intervention, however, the plan was abandoned and Dalip Singh focused instead on his social life in London. A member of the Garrick, the Marlborough, the East India Club, the Oriental Club and the Alhambra, he was also frequently spotted with various mistresses. By the time Sir Leslie Ward caricatured him as a portly, balding gentleman in 1882, he was widely known for his extramarital affairs.[18] The mounting expenses of an extravagant lifestyle, as well as those of his estate and family, led him to request an increase in his pension. The India Office refused, reigniting his old grievances about his confiscated kingdom. He went public in a letter to *The Times*, creating a rift between himself and the Queen. In 1886 he sailed to India with the intention of relocating there permanently and being reinitiated

Maharaja Dalip Singh
Sir Leslie Ward ('Spy'), 1882
Lithograph on paper
370 x 245 mm (14⅝ x 9⅝")
National Portrait Gallery,
London

into Sikhism. Intercepted at Aden by the British government, he nonetheless became a Sikh through the appropriate ceremonies.[19]

Dalip Singh was not allowed to return to India. While his family went back to Elveden, he settled instead in Paris, where he continued to rail against the British Government and plotted to reclaim the Punjab. Maharani Bamba died in 1887 even as his elaborate plan to take over his lost kingdom fell apart. Two years later he married Ada Douglas Weatherill, an Englishwoman with whom he had two daughters. He attempted to reconcile his differences with Queen Victoria, who eventually pardoned him in 1890. On 22 October 1893 the last Maharaja of the Punjab died in Paris; he was buried at his beloved Elveden.[20]

NOTES

1 Queen Victoria quoted in Alexander and Anand 1980, p. 45.

2 Jones 1999, p. 152; A.S. Madra, 'Singh, Dalip (1838–1893)', *Oxford Dictionary of National Biography*, Oxford University Press, September 2004; online edition January 2006 www.oxforddnb.com/view/article/41277, accessed 22 April 2006. Jones 1999, p. 153; Madra 2004; Bance 2004, pp. 14, 18–19.

3 Archer 1966, pp. 65–6. A similar portrait of the young king holding a gun (1840), attributed to the artist Imam Baksh, is in the collection of the Musée national des Arts Asiatiques – Guimet

(39750). See Jones 1999, p. 156.

4 M. Webster, 'Beechey, George Duncan (1797–1852)', *Oxford Dictionary of National Biography*, Oxford 2004 www.oxforddnb.com/view/article/1947, accessed 22 April 2006; Roberts 2002, p. 105. Emily Eden painted another larger picture of the Queen that was also gifted to Maharaja Ranjit Singh in November 1838. See Eden 1997, pp. 193, 201.

5 As recorded by Queen Victoria in her journal entry for 11 July 1854 and quoted in Axel 2001 p. 55. See also Alexander and Anand 1980, p. 46; B. Allen and C.A. Bayly, cat. 208 in Bayly 1990, p. 182.

6 Madra 2004; Jones 1999, p. 155; Rappaport 2003, pp. 228–31.

7 Bance 2004, p. 20; Aijazuddin 1979, pp. 74–7.

8 Letter from Queen Victoria to the Marquis of Dalhousie, Buckingham Palace, 26 July 1854, in Benson and Esher (eds) 1911, vol. 3, p. 39.

9 Bance 2004, pp. 28–9.

10 Bayly 1990, p. 182; Bance 2004, p. 28.

11 Axel 2001, p. 52.

12 Lord Dalhousie quoted in Bance 2004, p. 30.

13 Axel 2001, p. 56.

14 Bance 2004, p. 31; St-John Neville 1984, pp. 40–1, 45, 102.

15 Jones 1999, p. 158.

16 Bance 2004, p. 40.

17 Jones 1999, pp. 158–60; Bance 2004, p. 36; Madra 2004.

18 Bance 2004, pp. 46–7. Queen Victoria commented on the Maharaja's rotund figure in her journal entry recorded on 8 March 1880 at Windsor Castle. See St-John Neville 1984, p. 102.

19 Jones 1999, p. 162.

20 Madra 2004.

Bibliography

Aijazuddin, F.S. *Sikh Portraits by European Artists*, London, 1979

Alexander, M. and S. Anand, *Queen Victoria's Maharajah: Dalip Singh 1838–93*, New York, 1980

Archer, W.G. *Paintings of the Sikhs*, London, 1966

Axel, B.K. *The Nation's Tortured Body: Violence, Representation, and the Formation of a Sikh 'Diaspora'*, Durham, 2001

Bance, P. *The Dalip Singhs: The Photograph Album of Queen Victoria's Maharajah*, Phoenix Mill, Gloucestershire, 2004

Barratt, C.R. and E.G. Miles, *Gilbert Stuart*, exh. cat., The Metropolitan Museum of Art, New York, 2004

Bayly, C.A. (ed.), *The Raj: India and the British 1600–1947*, exh. cat., National Portrait Gallery, London, 1990

Beaglehole, J.C. (ed.), *The Journals of Captain James Cook on his Voyages of Discovery*, vol. 3: *The Voyage of the Resolution and Discovery, 1776–80*, Cambridge, 1967

Benson, A.C. and Viscount Esher (eds), *The Letters of Queen Victoria: A Selection from her Majesty's Correspondence Between the Years 1837 and 1861*, London, 1911

Bhabha, H.K. *The Location of Culture*, New York, 1994

Bond, R.P. *Queen Anne's American Kings*, Oxford, 1952

Brodsky, I. *Bennelong Profile*, Sydney, 1973

Calloway, C.G. *New Worlds for All: Indians, Europeans and the Remaking of Early America*, Baltimore and London, 1997

Challis, K. *Tales from Sydney Cove*, Sydney, 2000

Codell, J.F. and D.S. Macleod (ed.), *Orientalism Transposed: The Impact of the Colonies on British Culture*, Aldershot, 1998

Cohn, B.S. *Colonialism and Its Forms of Knowledge: The British in India*, Princeton, NJ, 1996

Colley. L. *Captives: Britain, Empire and the World 1600–1850*, London, 2003

Collins, D. *An Account of the English Colony of New South Wales (1798)*, Sydney, 1975

Connaughton, R. *Omai: The Prince Who Never Was*, King's Lynn, 2005

Cook and Omai: The Cult of the South Seas, exh. cat., National Library of Australia, Canberra, 2001

Cromwell Crawford, S. *Rammohan Roy: Social, Political and Religious Reform in 19th Century India*, New York, 1987

Dening, G. 'Ó Mai! This is Mai: A Masque of a Sort', in *Cook and Omai*, exh. cat., National Library of Australia, Canberra, 2001

Eden, E. *Up the Country: Letters Written to Her Sister from The Upper Provinces of India*, repr. London, 1997

Elsner, J. and J.-P. Rubiés (ed.), *Voyages and Visions: Towards a Cultural History of Trade*, London, 1999

Encounters: The Meeting of Asia and Europe 1500–1800, exh. cat., Victoria and Albert Museum, London, 2004

Fawcett Thompson, J.R. 'Thayendanegea the Mohawk and his Several Portraits. How the "Captain of the Six Nations" came to London and sat for Romney and Stuart', *Connoisseur*, no. 170 (1969), pp. 49–53

Fisher, M.H. *The First Indian Author in English: Dean Mahomed (1759–1851) in India, Ireland, and England*, Delhi, 1996, pp. 202–9

—— (ed.), *The Travels of Dean Mahomet: An Eighteenth-Century Journey Through India*, London, 1997

——, *Counterflows to Colonialism: Indian Travellers and Settlers in Britain 1600–1857*, Delhi, 2004

Foreman, C.T. *Indians Abroad, 1493–1934*, Norman, OK, 1943

Fryer, P. *Staying Power: The History of Black People in Britain*, London, 1984

Garratt, J.G. and B. Robertson, *The Four Indian Kings / Les Quatre Rois Indiens*, Ottawa, 1985

Gilbert, E.W. 'The Growth of Brighton', *Geographical Journal*, 114 (1/3) (July–September 1949), pp. 35–6

Gilbert, S. *Tattoo History: A Source Book*, New York, 2000

Grant, D. *The Fortunate Slave: An illustration of African slavery in the early eighteenth century*, London, 1968

Guest, H. 'Curiously Marked: Tattooing, Masculinity, and Nationality in Eighteenth Century British perceptions of the South Pacific', *Painting and the Politics of Culture: New Essays on British Art 1700–1850*, ed. J. Barrell, Oxford, 1992

Guthrie, N. '"No Truth or very little in the whole Story"? – A Reassessment of the Mohock Scare of 1712', *Eighteenth-Century Life*, 20, no. 2 (May 1996), pp. 33–56

Hackforth-Jones, J. 'Mai/Omai in London and the South Pacific: Performativity, Cultural Entanglement and Indigenous Appropriation', *Material Identities*, ed. J. Sofaer, Oxford, 2006

Hale, H. (ed.), *Brinton's Library of Aboriginal American Literature. Number II. The Iroquois Book of Rites*, Philadelphia, 1883

Hamilton, M.W. 'Joseph Brant – "The Most Painted Indian"', *New York History: The Quarterly Journal of New York State Historical Association*, 39, no. 2 (April 1958)

Haskell, F. *History and Its Images: Art and the Interpretation of the Past*, New Haven and London, 1995

Hinderaker, E. 'The "Four Indian Kings" and the Imaginative Construction of the First British Empire', *William and Mary Quarterly*, 3rd series, 53, no. 3 (July 1996), pp. 487–526

Honour, H. *The Image of the Black in Western Art*, vol. 4, part 2, Cambridge, MA, 1989

Hultkrantz, A. *Religions of the American Indians*, Berkeley, CA, 1981

Jones, D. 'Maharaja Dalip Singh', in S. Stronge (ed.), *The Arts of the Sikh Kingdoms*, New York, 1999

Kaeppler, A.L. *Artificial Curiosities: An Exposition of Native Manufactures Collected on the Three Pacific Voyages of Captain James Cook RN*, exh. cat., Bishop Museum, Honolulu, 1978

Kaplan, S. and E.N. Kaplan, *The Black Presence in the Era of the American Revolution*, Amherst, MA, 1989

Kenny, J. *Bennelong: First Notable Aboriginal*, Sydney, 1973

King, J.C.H. 'Collecting in the Context of Sloane's Catalogue of "Miscellanies"', in A. MacGregor (ed.), *Sir Hans Sloane: Collector, Scientist, Antiquary, Founding Father of the British Museum*, London, 1994, p. 229

——, *First Peoples, First Contacts: Native Peoples of North America*, Cambridge, MA, 1999

Klein, L. *Shaftesbury and the Culture of Politeness*, Cambridge, 1994

Kling, B.B. *Partner in Empire: Dwarkanath Tagore and the Age of Enterprise in Eastern India*, Berkeley, CA, 1976

Langlais Dodge, A.L. and S.S. Bean, 'Rediscovered: A Rare Portrait of Raja Rammohun Roy', *Marg* 52 ([1] September 2000), pp. 71–4

Lewis, R. *Gendering Orientalism: Race, Femininity and Representation*, London and New York, 1996

McCormick, E.H. *Omai Pacific Envoy*, Auckland, 1977

Mann, B.A. and J.L. Fields, 'A Sign in the Sky. Dating the League of the Haudenosaunee', in *American Indian Culture and Research Journal*, 21, no. 2 (1997), pp. 105–63

Nandy, A. *The Intimate Enemy: Loss and Recovery of Self Under Colonialism*, Delhi, 1983

O'Toole, F. *White Savage, William Johnson and the Invention of America*, London, 2005

Phillips, C. et al., *Ignatius Sancho: An African Man of Letters*, exh. cat., National Portrait Gallery, London, 1997

Pointon, M. *Hanging the Head: Portraiture and Social Formation in Eighteenth-Century England*, New Haven and London, 1993

Pomeroy, J. (ed.), *Intrepid Women: Victorian Artists Travel*, Aldershot, 2005

Pratt, S. 'Reynolds' "King of the Cherokees" and other mistaken identities in the portraiture of Native American delegations, 1710–1762', *Oxford Art Journal*, 21, no. 2 (1998),

Index